· ⌇ ·

MY VICTORIANS

· ⌇ ·

LOST
IN THE
NINETEENTH
CENTURY
**ROBERT
CLARK**

MY
VICTORIANS

UNIVERSITY
OF IOWA
PRESS
IOWA CITY

University of Iowa Press, Iowa City 52242
Copyright © 2019 by Robert Clark
www.uipress.uiowa.edu
Printed in the United States of America

Design by Kristina Kachele Design, llc

Printed on acid-free paper

Library of Congress Cataloging-in-Publication Data
Names: Clark, Robert, 1952– author.
Title: My Victorians : lost in the nineteenth century / Robert Clark.
Description: Iowa City : University of Iowa Press, [2019] |
Includes bibliographical references. |
Identifiers: LCCN 2019006687 (print) | LCCN 2019021847 (ebook) |
ISBN 978-1-60938-668-9 (ebook) | ISBN 978-1-60938-667-2 (paperback : alk. paper)
Subjects: LCSH: Clark, Robert, 1952– | Authors, American—20th century—
Biography. | Great Britain—Civilization—19th century.
Classification: LCC PS3553.L2878 (ebook) | LCC PS3553.L2878 Z63 2019 (print) |
DDC 818/.5403 [B] —dc23

LC record available at https://lccn.loc.gov/2019006687

For Kathy

CONTENTS

· ⌇ ·

INTRODUCTION

MY VICTORIANS are probably not your Victorians or anyone else's; nor, I'm pretty sure, are they by any stretch of the imagination the real Victorians—whoever they may have been. Mine are something else; let's call them evocative objects, affinities that took possession of me; things and persons that both awaken and then bewilder me, that seem likely to clarify but as often as not mystify, fascinating me for no apparent reason and drawing me in ways that feel sometimes perverse and compulsive, sometimes consoling and sustaining.

Perhaps I imagined that they would lead me deeper into myself. That, I think, is why over the course of several years—the last five, at least—I needed to pursue them, to make them the object of a quest. I aimed to track them down, reading, researching, returning to them again and again. At times I felt like a scholar or aficionado, at others like a stalker. I'm not sure I ever intended it to end or wanted it to. So if it was a quest, it might have been a quest without a goal, less a search than an evasion, a distraction that became a new life far away from the one I was stuck in.

There had been a marriage and a divorce; a religious conversion and an ebbing of faith; depression alternating with days just a little short of manic when I'd spend heedlessly on antique cameras, woolen scarves, fountain pens, and notebooks and tablets, not that they did anything to break the writer's block that also beset me. Then there was love and sex and relationships and all the chasms between them. I couldn't make sense of women, and I doubt they could make sense of me. I thought I was sensitive and kind and not bad looking, though perhaps I came off as simultaneously distant and importuning, smug and anxious; certainly I wasn't fun or sexy; I couldn't dance and didn't like to, which probably spoke volumes. I didn't so much relate to my dates as interview them. I would happily have skipped the drinks and conversation and read their dossiers instead. I still loved reading more than anything, the one thing in life that wasn't attended by worry or fear.

I've always had an appetite for catastrophe: tornados, nuclear devastation, imaginary wolves and rattlesnakes in the basement, but most of all plane crashes, tours de force of terror, annihilation, and gruesomeness, unimaginable things that I couldn't keep myself from imagining: the roller-coaster ride of descent; the fireball; the shattered, dismembered, and charred bodies.

It had to do with fear and uncertainty, of course, but also, I think, with a compulsive, repetitive need to see what shouldn't be seen. As a child the fact that such things could happen—that the world could be so unreliable and fragile and monstrous—terrified me, but I also found a sort of wonder in it, the discovery that things that seemed solid might come apart, that the sureties proclaimed by grown-ups were horrifically falsified. As an adult, I gradually came to put them further and further out of my mind. But the arrival of the internet opened new possibilities, easy access to fresh knowledge of my old fixations: a midair disintegration over Florida in 1963, a DC-10 that lost an engine and cartwheeled through the air before crashing in Chicago in 1979, but most of all the collision between two planes over New York harbor in 1960. I was eight years old, and I think that was the first crash whose totality I took in so that it took me in, thrust itself into my psyche and stayed alive there, a memory but also a persisting anxiety about something imminent, a smoldering dread. That's at the heart of what I wanted from the Victorian past, an escape from foreboding, from the sense that things might suddenly—would surely—fly apart. Perhaps I would find safety in books, history, biography, and, most of all, art—meanings that persist, that don't fall out of the sky. The past was immutable, open to interpretation, but settled, outside the reach of catastrophe in the present.

In the later Anglo-Catholic phase of his life, T. S. Eliot wrote in *Four Quartets*: "If all time is eternally present / All time is unredeemable." That for me was the heart of the matter. I, too, had just entered my Anglo-Catholic phase. Anglo-Catholicism itself was a Victorian development, a leap into the medieval past, aiming to restore the Catholic roots of the Protestant Church of England. It was one more way to immerse myself in the period. Though my faith had become nominal, a gesture rather than a commitment, I liked the services, the ceremony, the chants and vestments, the incense and solemnity. I wasn't going to be transformed by it, never mind redeemed, but it was beautiful. Of course, I would have been happy to have faith again: John Henry Newman, one of principal figures in Anglo-Catholicism (although he ultimately took the full plunge into the Roman church itself), quoting the Bible, said that faith was "the assurance of things hoped for." That for me would have meant nothing so much as a bulwark against catastrophe. It was the safe harbor of the undying past where you needn't fear Eliot's unredeemable time, the kind of time whose essence was change: flux, surprise, death. If I could have believed in it, eternal life would have solved everything.

So there it was: a menacing, capricious world breathing down my neck in the form of incomprehensible women, religion not so much felt as observed, incipient plane crashes. Ranged against all that, I would have the plotted certitudes of fat, episodic novels, Gothic revival liturgies, and women without caprice or troubling sorts of mystery, "angels of the house." I'd have wonder and discovery too, but in a realm of redeemed time where events and alterations couldn't touch me except in the ways I allowed them to, where each moment was a page in a book that moved toward foreseeable closures; love and marriage, inheritances, reunions, and redemptions—a different sort of assurance of things hoped for, knowing that all desires, cravings, and frustrations will be vanquished; then contentment, then blissful rest.

Some years earlier, I worked on another project pretty similar to this one. I was investigating my bloodlines, my genealogy, and discovered that I was related by either marriage or genes or both to Ralph Waldo Emerson, none too shabby an ancestry for a writer. I also discovered that Emerson had made a voyage to England in 1847. During his time there *Jane Eyre*, *Wuthering Heights*, *Vanity Fair*, and Christina Rossetti's first volume of poems were published; the Pre-Raphaelite Brotherhood of painters was formed; and Karl Marx and Friedrich Engels wrote *The Communist Manifesto* in London—a big chunk of the artifacts that for us constitute the Victorian age.

On the boat going over Emerson read the second volume of John Ruskin's *Modern Painters,* which had been published the previous year. Along with Thomas Carlyle, Ruskin was one of the two great Victorian sages, an art historian and critic who promoted J. M. W. Turner and the Pre-Raphaelites: Dante Gabriel Rossetti, John Everett Millais, and Holman Hunt and their acolytes, William Morris and Edward Burne-Jones. Raised Evangelical, Ruskin lost his faith but found a religion in art. He found a politics there too, a communitarian vision of a society founded not on economic competition but on the traditions of artisanship and cooperation.

Emerson and Ruskin were kindred spirits in their belief that the divine was to be found in nature rather than in traditional religion and also that it could be reified by human beings in the form of art. But where Emerson was confident and optimistic in these convictions, Ruskin was anxious, conflicted, and often tortured by doubts, inadequacies, and desires that his huge intelligence couldn't make sense of. He seemed to be a writer about art who himself enacted the artist's life; who, in Emerson's words, "spends himself, like the crayon in his hand, till he is all gone."

Once he arrived in England, Emerson seemed to meet everyone *except* Ruskin: he called on William Thackeray, Alfred Lord Tennyson, Benjamin Disraeli, William Wordsworth, Charles Dickens, George Eliot, Matthew Arnold, and, repeatedly, Thomas Carlyle. He strode through it all, impressed but not beguiled, sometimes amused by English insularity and its smug misapprehensions: "It was at Bridlington (pronounced Burlington) that one of the company asked me, if there were many rattlesnakes in the City of New York?"

By May 1848, after eight months, he'd had enough—he was an American, and the place oppressed him with bad dreams: "My Nights repeat my day, & I dream of gas light, heaps of faces, & darkness." He sailed home via Liverpool. Five years later, another ancient cousin of mine, Nathaniel Hawthorne, arrived and took over the consulate there. I'd been to Liverpool myself, although only once, to the Lever Museum across the Mersey to see its Pre-Raphaelite paintings. The museum has significant works by Millais, Hunt, and Rossetti, but the works by Burne-Jones were what drew me. Burne-Jones took the sensual languor of the first Pre-Raphaelite generation and transformed it into dreamscape, into oblivion, fleshly but disembodied, in the grip of a sexuality that doesn't know it wants consummation, held fast by longing that seems unaware of desire.

The painting that I stopped longest at was Burne-Jone's *The Beguiling of Merlin*, the kind of Arthurian medieval story that the Victorians loved, suggesting a better, more heroic English past but also one darker and more tragic, in which nature and humankind have yet to make peace with one another; a world in which haunted people transit a haunted world. In the painting, Merlin has been put under a spell by the Lady of the Lake, with whom he's infatuated. He is supine and has managed to lift one shoulder but no more, as if a chain or the weight of his sleep is holding him fast. She looks into his eyes as he looks back sidelong, his gaze at once transfixed and narcoleptic. But he can't raise himself up—can't go further—or, perhaps, *won't* raise himself up. He's infatuated twice over, moved by her female sexuality but also immobilized by it. There's magic and enthrallment, desire and paralysis, life that feels like afterlife, an eternal laudanum-like stupor. It's as though in the absence of a God this limbo—heaven overlapping hell—is the most likely end that the Victorian soul can imagine.

Looking back, it seems that what I call my Victoromania had something of that quality. Reading Victorian novels—easily more than a hundred—plus histories, biographies, letters, and diaries, I cocooned myself; lost track of time over maps of nineteenth-century railroads and slums; hypnotized myself gazing at the pages of books of Victorian art and architecture.

My obsessions didn't stop there: I planned to visit and photo-graph every house that my favorite writers had lived in as well as the settings of their books. I'd go to railway stations and churches too, because they constituted the bulk of Victorian architecture and because I was still making myself go to church: like the Victorians, I was also struggling with "difficulties," but I meant to go through the motions of religion, just in case, as Dickens put it, something would turn up. I even considered trying a dose of laudanum, the Victorians' analgesic and soporific of choice, but couldn't find one, at least not without the services of a prescribing doctor and a chemist to compound it.

Unlike Emerson, I couldn't get enough of England, admittedly not England as it is, but as it was. When I began to travel there two and sometimes three times a year for weeks (several times for months), my friends at home in Seattle saw that it was in the antic-ipation of these trips that I came fully alive. When they asked why, I would always say that going to England was like being inside my favorite books. I was making, it seems to me now, an imaginary room—walls, floor, and ceiling—of novels: all of the three Brontë sisters, all of Wilkie Collins, all of George Gissing, all of Charles Dickens, a massive if incomplete reading of Elizabeth Gaskell, Mary Ward, and many, many more. Then I could hang its walls with pictures by Burne-Jones and Millais and the photos I took of brick walls and brass-knockered red doors. There was no end to Victorians and their relics: I needn't stop at a room; I could build a whole place to live, my house of oblivion. I would labor at it in the compulsive and encyclopedic manner of two of my favorite novels' manic obsessive characters, *David Copperfield*'s Mr. Dick and *Middlemarch*'s Edward Casaubon. I'd feed the fireplace until all that was solid melted into the coal-smoked air. I'd spend myself, like a crayon in my hand, till I was all gone, at peace, redeemed.

Chapter 1

ON JUNE 20, 1853, the painter John Everett Millais, the critic John Ruskin, and Ruskin's wife, born Euphemia Grey but universally known as Effie, set off for Scotland. Ruskin intended to teach Millais to paint landscape and water ("You shall see things as they Are," Ruskin liked to say). Millais planned to paint twin portraits of the Ruskins, while Effie—let's call her by her first name; she's the inspiration and the helpmate, the watcher and the watched—would sketch and embroider and read novels.

You may know something of their story: the Ruskins and their unconsummated marriage and the affair of Effie and Millais, which Ruskin may well have greeted with relief and may even, with his parents' help, have connived at. She had known since their honeymoon that Ruskin didn't want her ("the reason he did not make me his Wife was because he was disgusted with my person the first evening 10th April [1848]"); she saw that he was always elsewhere ("John is spending all his money on Missals—he has a perfect mania in that line just now"), writing the next volume of *Modern Painters* or *The Stones of Venice*, sketching rocks and outcroppings.

Myself, I have seen any number of drawings, paintings, and photos of Effie, and she seems attractive enough. She had broad, rather narrow eyes and a long elegant nose and looks a little sly—not devious, but as though she might laugh at any moment (especially if you were being overly serious), as though she might suddenly tease you, maybe flirtatiously. And while my character is a bit like Ruskin's (I have manias; I'm a bit frayed around the edges of my psyche; a little fond of solitude, wary of parties and crowds, of bodies and intimacy), I'd date Effie in an instant. I'd go moony over her, as Millais did over both of them at first: "The Ruskins *are most perfect people. . . .* She is the most delightful unselfish kind hearted creature I ever knew, it is impossible to help liking her—he is gentle and forbearing." This is from a letter that he wrote to his best friend, the painter Holman Hunt, from Glenfinlas at Brig O'Turk in the Trossachs, near Loch Lomond, the deep imaginary of Sir Walter Scott's novels, where they settled in for three months at the beginning of July.

I decided to visit Glenfinlas, but first I wanted to see everything connected with the summer of 1853: drawings by Ruskin and sketches, studies, and of course paintings by Millais. The bulk of it was in the Ashmolean Museum in Oxford: Ruskin's drawing of the gneiss rock along the river; Millais's studies of Ruskin standing amid waterfalls on the same formation; and the finished portrait.

In the library, they gave me white cotton gloves to wear and let me handle the drawings, chiefly Ruskin's *Study of Gneiss*, which took a kind of possession of me. It was uniformly gray, a lampblack wash and pen over pencil. There was vegetation along the upper edge—ferns, honeysuckle, a spindly ash tree—but nothing but rock below, sloping toward the lower right corner, striated in the same direction, globular, as though it had melted and run, pooling in a horizontal lobe at the bottom.

John Ruskin, *Study of Gneiss Rock, Glenfinlas* (1853). By permission of the Ashmolean Museum, University of Oxford, UK/Bridgeman Images.

That doesn't sound like much, and perhaps the formation itself is nothing remarkable. But Ruskin bore down microscopically on its particulars, gave them a kind of attention that for me made the whole almost impossibly vivid—something that was not present when I saw the actual formation, whereas in the drawing it seemed to leap out at me, compelling me to see it in a way I had previously been incapable of seeing.

Downstairs in the main gallery, I stood a long time before Millais's portrait of Ruskin. Ruskin is in a frock coat, a high collar and tie, and tapered gray trousers that lap the tops of his sleek black shoes, holding what at the time would have been considered a casual brown hat—none of it casual by our standards. He's looking downstream, half in reverie, half watching; *seeing*, as he would have it. There's a green and chestnut cast to the overall hue of the painting, and you can unmistakably make out the gneiss formation that Ruskin drew. The rendering of the water, which was one of the points of the expedition, is not—to my eye—entirely successful: the foam and eddies look more like stratus clouds than pooling water and the waterfalls curtain down statically rather than roiling and pouring. Ruskin, who took Millais to Scotland to help him master painting it, did better in his own drawing of gneiss.

Still, it's a good painting. Millais was, for my money, the best of the Pre-Raphaelites; the least mannered and willfully eccentric, the most technically competent. Crucially, to me, he had a grasp of emotional truth, not just of Ruskin's "true-to-nature" imperative but of human tenderness. He had a gift for portraying women and girls that avoided both the vampery of Rossetti's "stunners" and the Technicolor hyperrealism (save for the faces and heads) of his friend Holman Hunt.

I have, truth be told, mostly mixed feelings about the Pre-Raphaelites. I love the dreaminess, the narcoticized erotic that begins in Rossetti and ends, beautifully, in Burne-Jones. But then there's the stuff that makes me cringe, paintings that make my teeth hurt, cloying, candy-colored, earnest, and amateurish—wincingly corny by the lights of the twenty-first century. The painting that epitomizes this for me was also in Oxford, at Keble College: Holman Hunt's *The Light of the World*, the most popular painting of the Victorian age. People stood in line, rooted, stunned and weeping before it. It was endlessly reproduced, and Hunt himself made two more versions of it.

I went to see it that same day, after leaving the Ashmolean. In part, I went to find out if I could stand it, if I could see anything to like in it or at least to understand. I didn't want to mock it or hold it in contempt: I had, I liked to think, a broad sympathy for the Victorians; they fascinated me as the missals, rocks, and Turners fascinated Ruskin. I wanted to meet them halfway, to comprehend what they saw in it, even if I saw very little.

There was another reason to see it, which I only became aware of later: *The Light of the World* was the painting that Hunt was working on at the same time Millais was working on Ruskin's portrait. Moreover, Millais and Hunt had a passionate friendship, which we would be inclined to pathologize much as we do the taste of the people who loved *The Light of the World*. Hunt was, in fact, meant to join Millais and the Ruskins on the expedition to Scotland. Millais openly wept and keened when he learned that Hunt couldn't make it, too busy traveling to the Holy Land and working on *The Light of the World*.

We like to categorize Victorian desire within our categories, not theirs, so we believe that it was always repressed and constructed by forces they couldn't—unlike us—reflect on; they couldn't, despite Ruskin, see things straight. That goes doubly for Ruskin himself: How could he reject Effie in favor of virginity or aestheticism or whatever it was? Most of the proffered explanations are risible (chiefly that he couldn't bear the sight of her pubic hair), but without any resort to theory I wonder the same thing—merely on account of Effie's beauty, on the basis of my own attraction. Ruskin's rejection of her seems as incomprehensible as liking *The Light of the World*; maybe it's even somehow the same thing.

I'd seen *The Light of the World* twenty-five years ago on loan to the Tate Gallery and described it in an essay as "an exaltation of corn

. . . Jesus with his lantern, trick-or-treating for souls on Pumpkin Night . . . you die of embarrassment." I'd like to say that I was now less smug, but when I got to the Keble College chapel where the painting sits behind a rope, illuminated by a timed spot that you ignite by pressing a button, I still couldn't bear it. It was smaller than I imagined or remembered, and I thought the size—so much awfulness in a tiny package—made it even more absurd. And I saw now that one of its main absurdities was the size of Christ's head, which—allowing for perspective (which Hunt was generally pretty good at)—was smaller than the lamp he carried. That his head was surmounted by a crown and his chin festooned with a russet beard made it that much worse. I took a selfie—maybe selfies are to us what *The Light of the World* was to Victorians: transfixing, essential, an anchor in a fragmented world. I didn't have to feign my distaste. But then there were the eyes: sad, confused, deprived of any triumphalism or even much confidence. I knew the theological reasons why Christ might look that way—that in order to bring this light into the world he will have to suffer and die; still more, that the people he's bringing it to are as likely as not to reject it—but I was mainly flummoxed: in those two inches or so, there was something that felt very much like truth, like something previously unseen made visible, into art. The eyes might have even fit our contemporary definition of art—shock and awe undergone in a museum—because they were troubling, impossible to parse if you gave the painting half a chance, if the scales dropped from your own eyes.

When I'd left my home in Seattle for England, I had more in mind than research. I'd been divorced five years and been dating online but without much success. But in London, I thought, I might have better luck: with my interests and in a large population center full of artists, intellectuals, scholars, and writers, there ought to be more suitable types than I found in Seattle and not a few fellow Victorianists. That was the card I played most heavily when I posted a profile on the dating site of the *Guardian*:

William Holman Hunt, *The Light of the World* (c. 1851–53).
By permission of the Warden and Fellows of Keble College,
Oxford/Bridgeman Images.

I'm American, a transatlantic commuter, not exactly an innocent abroad but, despite quite a few years resident in Europe, someone whose midwestern roots show in the manner of one of F. Scott Fitzgerald's *Gatsby* characters: naivety bruised but with a capacity for wonder still intact, rowing sometimes unwisely against the current.

I'm an author (of both novels and nonfiction) and teach creative writing in a university MFA course, and I'm pretty free to live where and how I please, generally depending on whatever writing project I'm pursuing. My latest obsession is Victoriana, or really Victoromania, chiefly my own, which has crept up on me over the last decade and seems in many ways inexplicable but extends to art, architecture, novels, Ruskin, Gissing, Dickens, Gaskell, C. Rossetti, trains and ruins, etc. (Also recently crazy about Forster, Mansfield, Bowen, Taylor.) I'm open to putting down deeper roots in England: my ancestors emigrated from Suffolk and London 300 years ago, but what's a few years' hiatus? At present, I'm here about six months a year, but should I meet someone special . . .

I've been divorced five years, I'm fit, and my photos were all taken within the last eighteen months. I'm politically progressive and a diffident Anglo-Catholic, but will only mention the latter if asked, though I do like to visit churches. I'm introverted but not cripplingly so, sybaritic when it comes to food and wine, and, so I'm told, quite funny. Need music (classical, art song, much more), films, espresso, wine, humor, and books to function, and—who knows?—maybe you. You don't have to wear a bonnet and muslin but I wouldn't mind if you were pretty, fit, and happy in your vocation and busy finding your heart's desire.

I hadn't quite thought through what would happen if anyone responded—if I was really prepared to move 5,000 miles for the right person—but I was joining the site on a lark, with no expectations, or so I told myself. If anyone replied, I'd be clear about my situation and at least I might make a friend.

But there were quite a few responses, particularly from art historians, museum curators, and scholars and fans of Victorian history, literature, and art. I'd imagined my own Victoromania to be a pretty singular thing; maybe, in truth, I liked it that way. It made me special and, if eccentric, eccentric in my own fashion; in— when you got down to it—a Victorian way. Now I had discovered that I wasn't alone; reading their e-mails and gazing at their photos, I saw that there were women I could share my obsession with and maybe become lovers too. Victoromania plus companionship plus sex: for these I would compromise my eccentricity. And if I had no luck, I'd still have my solitude, my books and camera, my private world.

My first date was with a feminist art historian, Annie, not exactly a Victorianist but funny and incisive. We bantered and laughed a lot on our first two dates, though she was a bit incredulous when I mentioned that I taught writing at a church-affiliated university. She wondered what sort of nonsense I believed; still more, how art and the creative process could be taught and flourish in such an environment. I hastened to explain that I wasn't one of *them*, that when I'd applied for the job I'd suggested otherwise, played along, gone through the motions. In fact, on the job application and contract I'd pretty happily assented to the bulk of Christian dogma without much compunction, knowing that any number of adherents struggled with the same doubts. I didn't quite believe but I didn't quite not believe, not enough to renounce it in a thoroughgoing way—except over dinner with an attractive woman. I'd let her construe whatever she wanted about my not being one of them. If she pressed me further, I'd tell myself and her that I was being nuanced rather than evasive. Art, among other things, was surely about nuance.

On our second date we'd done some passionate kissing in her car when she dropped me off at my flat. So this date, our third, might culminate in something, cement us or undo us. That was the night of the day I'd gone to Oxford and communed with Ruskin, Millais, and Holman Hunt.

I gave her a full report, showing her my dyspeptic selfie in front of *The Light of the World*, and we had a good laugh. But what I went on about was Ruskin's *Study of Gneiss*. She looked at the shot I'd taken of it on my phone and shook her head: "He didn't add anything with this, didn't advance art in any way." It was an illustration, a meticulous rendering that was no more than the sum of its parts.

I argued with her. I said that maybe she was partially right: it was photographic, everything was foreground, and that represented a way of seeing that was strange and new at the time. It was Ruskin's own dictum of truth-to-nature, of "seeing things as they Are," made manifest. He'd argued, in fact, that no kind of observation was more fundamental to art than geology:

[The laws of the organization of the earth] are in the landscape the foundation of all other truths—the most necessary, therefore, even if they were not in themselves attractive; but they are as beautiful as they are essential, and every abandonment of them by the artist must end in deformity as it begins in falsehood.

But Annie was unswayed and, I sensed, impatient. I went back to *The Light of the World* in hopes of easing the mood, but to not much effect: we'd already been over that, and the evening had seized up at some earlier moment. I didn't bring up the Hunt eyes, of course.

When she dropped me off, we didn't kiss. We met a week later. Over dinner I also told her that I was going back to America in two weeks, something that I was sure I'd already mentioned—that I'd made explicit. She said, though, that I'd misled her about my intentions. She looked angry and also hurt; she'd felt something, which was something I hadn't planned on. I never heard from her again.

He's made me real, Effie seemed to say when Millais first painted her in *The Order of Release*. In 1851 the Ruskins had visited Millais's house in Gower Street—the birthplace of the Pre-Raphaelite Brotherhood—in the wake of Ruskin's influential letters to the *Times* in defense of the movement. They'd stayed in touch, and in early 1853 Ruskin suggested that Effie pose for Millais's entry in that year's Royal Academy Exhibition. Writing a friend about the finished painting, *The Order of Release*, Effie said, "My head you would know anywhere. In fact it is exactly like . . . absurdly like; any body who has ever seen me once would remember it was somebody they knew."

There are five figures in the picture: A Jacobite prisoner of war, his guard, a dog, Effie, and the infant she's holding. No faces are fully visibly except hers. The theme of the painting—the reunion of the Jacobite rebel with his wife and child—would seem to dictate that her expression be overcome by emotion, by tears or joy. But she's impassive, not nonplussed but cryptic, inscrutable. Millais's faces of women are like this: from his *Ophelia* two years earlier to his portrait of Effie's sister Sophie four years later, these women are not quite present but suspended in moments of intense but unreadable feeling; maybe on the near or far verge of consciousness—dreams, sleep, shock—but, to me, refusing to be read, to reveal themselves, to be seen.

You can say that this has little to do with his sitters and everything to do with how Millais saw and felt about women; that he found something threateningly sphinx-like in them or, alternatively, something erotically compelling in such expressions, which elicit neither approach or rejection, which are fundamentally and profoundly self-contained. Maybe he saw this especially in Effie—perhaps because that was how Effie really was, "exactly like," as she put it herself.

Ruskin seems to have seen the same thing but knew even less than Millais what to make of it. He made a sketch of Effie in Verona in 1850, when the two of them were two-years-married virgins. He drew it in sanguine, the red chalk favored by Renaissance artists. Despite that color it's scarcely visible: pale, diaphanous, bounded by neither line nor shadow, as though Effie were a ghost or a phantasm. Or perhaps Ruskin simply gave up: went as far as the suggestion of a drawing and no further. There's no more than the faint outline of her pulled-back hair, the tight slits of her eyes, and her mouth, made not for speaking but for reproach, for refusal; stringent and, like the eyes, implacable. And that's all. That's as far as he got or preferred to go. I don't think that her person disgusted him but that it confounded him.

One other Ruskin drawing seems remarkably similar: his self-portrait of 1873, twenty years after the Scottish expedition. Charles Eliot Norton, one of the most prominent American intellectuals of his time as well as an art history professor at Harvard, was one of Ruskin's closest friends and asked him for a likeness. It is not the kind of self-rendering that most people would send on such an occasion. Ruskin is glaring, almost scowling. His blue eyes are overhung by fierce brows with a creased forehead above them and a hawk-like nose below. The mouth is small and tight. The left side of his face is in shadow, the gouache scored as though his cheek's been scratched or clawed. It would take most any friend aback; it would frighten a child. Ten years later Norton would write a lecture series called "The Storm Cloud of the Nineteenth Century"—and here it is, in a face.

Comparing the drawing to contemporary photographs of Ruskin, it is arguably not a perfect likeness in the way that Effie meant in regard to Millais's painting of her. In the photos, Ruskin doesn't look so old, so reduced to a pair of eyes raking the viewer with his gaze, his desire to "see things as they Are" concentrated into a death-ray. Perhaps it was people in general that stymied him, including himself. But not in this self-portrait: some variety of emotion is unmistakable and overwhelming. Of that work, I would tell my art-historian date, "No, this changes everything."

I came back the following spring to go north to Scotland and brought my camera. During the two weeks before I left London, I bought everything there was to read about the Ruskins and Millais. I went to Oxford for the second time and reviewed everything I'd seen before, not least the *Study of Gneiss*, which had lost none of its power over me. The curator in the print room also brought me a sketch that I hadn't seen before, which she thought might be of interest. It's of Effie, not by Ruskin but by Millais; though it is undated, Effie is young: her hair is in the style she wore that summer, the same as in numerous other sketches made by Millais that are known to have been made at Glenfinlas. It's a profile, so I couldn't see both her eyes or her full mouth, but there's no sign of the piercing gaze of Ruskin's 1850 drawing. I decided that, yes, it was drawn in Scotland in 1853 and that she was in love.

Millais spent all his time drawing her as soon as he and the Ruskins arrived in Scotland at the end of June. Millais immediately wrote Hunt: "Today I have been drawing Mrs Ruskin who is the sweetest creature that ever lived." Ruskin, too, was "benign and kind." So Millais felt contented despite desperately missing Hunt as well as being continually beset by midges, which turned his skin leprous. Millais was tall, spindly, and not a little sickly, but forever joyfully amazed that the world was so lovely and that the people in it were kind to him, "compassionated" him, in Victorian diction.

By July 4 they had reached Glenfinlas by way of Doune Castle, where Millais had the idea of posing Effie for a portrait next to a window that would make a diptych with the one of Ruskin that he'd already planned. Three days later they had found the setting for the latter: "Millais has fixed on his place," Ruskin wrote his father, "a lovely piece of worn rock, with foaming water, and weeds, and moss, and a noble overhanging bank of dark crag— and I am to be standing looking quietly down the stream—just the sort of thing I used to do for hours."

Brig O'Turk schoolmaster's cottage. Photograph by author.

They stayed in the local hotel for a week and then rented the Brig O'Turk schoolmaster's cottage, further up the glen and closer to the portrait site. The quarters were tight—a living room where Ruskin worked and slept on the couch—and two alcoves, not much bigger than ship bunks, for Effie and Millais. Ruskin's valet was also there; Millais's brother William joined them later for several weeks.

While waiting for the canvas he'd ordered for the portrait, Millais painted Effie on a smaller scale as she sat, eyes cast down at her "work," which in Victorian usage meant "needlework"—mending, embroidering, or sewing—the only sort of "work" a woman of Effie's class might be imagined doing. Otherwise at leisure, she'd also read and sketch. This is how she occupied herself both in the schoolmaster's cottage and in the glen where Millais was making studies for the portrait.

Ruskin often remained in the cottage, compiling an eighty-page index for his three-volume *The Stones of Venice* and also preparing a lecture series on Turner that was to be given in Edinburgh in the autumn. In the evenings Ruskin read to her and Millais from Sir Walter Scott's *Guy Mannering*. He and Millais played shuttlecock over the dining table, ferocious engagements that could last an hour.

But otherwise Ruskin was not quite there, not quite among them. The plan for the portrait had always been to pose him gazing downstream contemplating what he saw or lost in deep thought or some combination of the two, looking "not of our kind," as he seemed to Millais in a letter to Hunt: "His soul is always with the clouds and out of reach of ordinary mortals—I mean that he theorises about the vastness of space and looks at a lovely little stream in practical contempt."

In the same letter Millais mentioned the companion portrait of Effie that he was planning to do at Doune Castle: "I am going to paint her at a window overlooking a river and distant mountains with a view of Stirling Castle." But that painting was never made or even started. Instead, he painted her in the glen as she sketched and then again in the cottage, at her work with foxgloves braided into her hair.

I think Millais's foxglove portrait is the image of Effie I like best. The pose is identical to the one Millais painted at roughly the same date by the waterfall; in fact, looking closely, I'd say she's wearing the same clothes and is working on the same sewing in both paintings. By the waterfall, she's wearing a hat, so I don't know if the foxgloves were there that day too. And then I wonder who wove them into her hair. She didn't have a maid with her, and it seems a tricky job to do in the mirror. Was it Millais? It seems terribly intimate, insinuating your fingers in someone's hair with the deliberation it would take to get it right, looking at her hair so intently, touching her in so particular and delicate a way. And who picked them and suggested weaving them into Effie's hair? Picking flowers was the kind of thing Millais was inclined to do: I picture him bringing the flowers to Effie and their coming up with the idea of doing this together, of entangling themselves.

A week later, Millais took a hard fall in the glen, injuring his nose and crushing his thumb, which Effie recorded in her diary: "He got quite pale and I led him home as best I could. He lent on me all the way and it was dreadful pain between his nose and his thumb." She bandaged the thumb and held his throbbing hand. After the pain had eased and the nail sloughed off, she tended his hair: "I have a drawing of myself cutting his Hair at that time in the little Cottage where he has traced the bar across his nose and I think also his wounded thumb." She capitalized "hair" and "cottage," and I wonder about that, too.

Perhaps I'm making too much of all this. In any case, Millais gave the foxglove painting to Ruskin, who was pleased with it. He asked his father to order a presentation set of *The Stones of Venice* specially bound in dark green for Millais. He "has been making me innumerable presents of little sketches and a beautiful painting of Effie with foxgloves in her hair—worth at least £50. I should like the books done with silk inside."

So Ruskin didn't seem to mind these intimacies in the least. His aim had been to make a better painter of Millais, which seemed to be happening according to plan. And though we can't know—Ruskin was "not of our kind"—rather than simply not being able to see what was going on (his sight was acute but selective), perhaps he in fact wanted Effie to have a lover, someone to take her off his hands. Maybe Millais knew this in some inchoate way or was simply lost in his infatuation. He'd begun to call her "The Countess," not because she was imperious but because she was a pearl beyond price. In another letter to Hunt, he exulted over what

John Everett Millais, *Portrait of Effie with Foxgloves* (1853).
Private collection. Photo © Peter Nahum at the Leicester
Galleries, London/Bridgeman Images.

a prize Effie was and seemed to be imagining how things might go
if they could be alone together: "You really have cause to be jealous of Mrs. Ruskin for a more delightful creature never breathed.
If I could meet with her . . . "

Hunt might have been a little jealous, might envy him, but Ruskin apparently did not. Ruskin was merely conscious of a certain happy agitation in Millais, his pupil: "I don't know how to manage him, his mind is so *terribly* active. . . . He cannot go on in this way." Fortunately, the large canvas—gessoed bright white in the Pre-Raphaelite manner—arrived. On July 28 Millais began.

Once the work was underway, Millais drew pictures of himself at work on the portrait or, really, of him and Effie sitting by his side, holding a book, reading to him. From another letter to Hunt, we know that she was reading him Dante; about hell, purgatory, and heaven, but in any case about suffering and loving, desire upon which the whole creation seems to move. The odd thing about this drawing as we have it today from among Effie's effects is that the whole upper right corner has been cut out: the place where Ruskin would have been standing. Ruskin has been excised, and she and Millais are indeed alone. It seems likely that it was she who removed him.

In other sketches, Millais drew himself and Effie huddling close together under a coat, defending themselves against the perpetual rain and midges. He looks downcast and frail—his hand is still bandaged—while she scans the path ahead. It seems she's holding his arm. In another, he's teasing her, brushing and tickling her face with a fern. Millais put Ruskin in this one, looking on with a smile, deeply amused. When Millais's brother William visited them, he later recollected that Ruskin usually sent Millais and Effie off together while he and William talked or Ruskin worked: "[He] preferred that E.C.G. [Effie] should roam the hills with J.E.M. [Millais]—and frequently they didn't return until quite late—Ruskin's remark to me was, 'How well your brother & my wife get on together.' "

Perhaps it had nothing to do with the time Millais was devoting to Effie, but progress on Ruskin's portrait was slow in relation to the speed at which he had dashed off sketches and small canvases of Effie. In the first ten days he managed two inches of paint, "a most exquisite piece of leafage," Ruskin (more concerned with truth-to-nature than expediency) wrote to his father. As often as not the weather was terrible, and Millais wrote to Hunt (who was taking just as long with *The Light of the World*), complaining of being stuck in the cottage. But he had Effie to draw, now putting her in historic scenes of Scottish and classical history. He also began to sketch her in costumes—not just dresses but headgear and accessories—that may have been imaginary or may have been fabricated in the cottage. Effie loved to dress up and Millais liked to admire her, and in each drawing she becomes more precisely defined, more beautiful, more palpable.

I look at the sketches and feel drawn to her. Her nose no longer seems to me the least bit vulpine. It's elegant, and Millais has filled out her lips. She's still enigmatic, not to be trifled with, as grave, perhaps sad, as she is self-possessed, but I could see wanting her. He's done the same with her body. The usual cloak or shawl has been stripped away so that you can see the shape of her breasts, waist, and hips. He's drawn ribbons falling down her back and buttons up her front, large and prominent enough that you could imagine them being unfastened, watching the whole ensemble fall away.

Writing these things, I wonder if I am little odd, maybe even perverse. Because she's close to two centuries older than me, and because everything I know about her is in the hearsay of other men's images of her and in a few letters, diaries, and legal statements: that "the reason he did not make me his Wife was because he was disgusted with my person the first evening 10th April [1848]." According to the doctor's report filed in support of her motion for annulment, "we found the usual signs of virginity and that she is naturally and properly formed."

That second quotation takes me aback: the humiliation and invasion of the doctor's examination and that I am privy to it and not a little fascinated by it. It marks her as being more of a girl than a full-fledged woman. But it is also somehow a marker of her self-possession: she is "intact" in the conventional Victorian sense but also within herself, an agent rather than an object. And that may have something to do with how she seems in Millais's art.

This is true as far as it goes, but the truth in relation to my fascination may lie elsewhere. Because, really, I'm attracted, fascinated, but also confused, both drawn to her and afraid. And in that I'm nothing so much as Victorian. I want her covered up and I want her naked. I want the imperturbable woman who needs to be known on her own terms, but perhaps I also, like Ruskin, want her to be a girl whom I could cajole and shape. Drawn to the person I see but don't truly comprehend—and that's half the attraction—my impulse is to simplify her, to strip off what drew me in the first place.

After ten days of work, Ruskin thought the painting was going well and would "be peculiarly beautiful because there is no *sun* in it":

> all dark rocks with plants hanging down over them and the foaming water below—and [Millais] paints so brightly that he cannot possibly have too quiet a subject. I am drawing art of the rocks close to him and Effie reads to us, or draws separate plants for flowers for practice.

As far as Ruskin was concerned, it was as fine as fine could be: the right light, and all of them making art, he himself doing the *Study of Gneiss*. But it was otherwise with Millais. Writing again to Hunt he says, "I feel very tired . . . and low spirited, I don't receive gratification from scarcely anything. The only pleasure is teaching Mrs. Ruskin drawing, she is such a delightful creature." Nor, despite Ruskin's vocal and unstinting enthusiasm, did he have anything to say about his own work, although he was eager to know about Hunt's: "Tell me what you are painting and have you finished the Moonlight?" (his name for *The Light of the World*). By the end of August he was telling Hunt that "it would be quite impossible to stay here if it were not for Mrs. Ruskin who is more

Glenfinlas. Photograph by author.

delightful every day." A week later, he wrote that "I am sure I don't know what else to say except it be that I am painting rocks perpetually. . . . Mrs Ruskin goes on like an 'Express' with painting and I don't sleep very well at night and am sure if my face in the slightest degree told of my restlessness and suffering, it would be lined like a Bradshaw railway map."

Hunt had now presold the still unfinished *The Light of World* for 400 guineas (in excess of £40,000 in today's money), but, as Ruskin wrote over a succession of days in early October, Millais's future would exceed that success if the portrait was any indicator:

Millais has put all his strength into the ash bough at the top of the picture—and the dark rocks and creepers below this. Nothing can be finer. . . .

Millais has done some glorious bits of rock these last two or three days with all their lichens gleaming like frosted silver—most heavenly. . . .

Millais' picture is beginning to surpass even my expectations—the lichens are coming out upon the purple rocks like silver chasing on a purple robe and the water—which I was nervous about is quite perfect—truly such as never was painted before.

There was no sense of these perfections apparent in what Millais wrote Hunt the same day: "I believe I shall kill myself for the cold and the damp is intense . . . so long to finish this background but I fear it will take me three weeks more at least. . . . This is a little writched [*sic*] picture." But then there was Effie's account of "the cold and damp" in a letter written to a friend the day after that:

the other evening you would have been sorry for me: I was returning home with Millais and coming to a very dirty mud bank I asked his help; it was quite dark and he told me to walk on the edge of the grass and I thought I was getting home nicely. He had fast hold of my arm, when my feet went from under me and down I fell into a cold mud bath. He fell too partly upon me but thereby served himself, but when I got pulled up I found by my weight how much it had been added to by my fall, and on reaching home I found myself in such a state my frock could not be brushed for two days.

I read this and see that Effie was a trouper, tending the men, shouting over the thunder of the glen, marching through bogs and up mud banks. She's a writer, too; deft at irony in her coy "you would have been sorry for me," asking for a sympathy that she neither needs nor wants as she falls: falls into Millais's arms.

Shrouded in mud, soaked through, she might have been embarrassed beyond words, but I can't help but think that the intimacy was that much closer for the two of them being so humbled, so stripped of dignity and pretense; naked, so to speak, and entangled "in such a state."

At the end of the letter, Effie adds that in two weeks she and Ruskin will be "leaving Mr. Millais here as his Picture is not done." This threw Millais into a tailspin that Ruskin could no longer ignore.

> I don't know how to manage him and he does not know how to manage himself... won't, or can't, eat any breakfast or dinner.
> ... Sometimes he is all excitement, sometimes depressed and faint as a woman, always restless and unhappy. I think I never saw such a miserable person on the whole. . . . The faintness seems so excessive, sometimes appearing almost hysterical.

Millais was obviously lovesick: he has seen what any man—or at least me—would see in Effie. Crazily (or perhaps aptly), it has rendered him "a woman" and made him "hysterical." He needs Effie, unruffled and unflappable, to tend him, but now she's leaving him in the Scottish muck and cold to finish a painting of her abstracted, rock and lichen–obsessed husband.

Then there's Hunt: having completed the background of *The Light of the World*, he is at last sailing for the Middle East. As Millais wrote to him, "scarcely a night passes but what I cry like an infant over the thought that I may never see you again." Ruskin (and perhaps he deserves more credit than I've been giving him) did know about this side of Millais's lovesickness and wrote Hunt a concerned letter: "I can't help writing you tonight; for here is [Millais] crying on his bed like a child—or rather with that bitterness that is only in a man's grief—and I don't know what will become of him when you are gone." Ruskin then begged Hunt to cancel his journey and come succor Millais. "*I* can be of no use to him—he has no sympathy with me or my ways."

In this letter, Ruskin displays not only genuine concern but unexpected insight. He understands that Millais has no "sympathy" with him—does not, in our parlance, relate to him. He also nails something that goes to the core of male experience: "that bitterness that is only in a man's grief": not just loss and sorrow, but a rage at being made vulnerable by them. I've felt it myself, exactly that, especially in love, and I'm taken aback that Ruskin—a man who incomprehensibly wanted to be a virgin—comprehends it. Or maybe he's strangely like Effie in this one facet: somehow sharper, wiser, more visionary on account of being enclosed in the boundaries he's chosen. Maybe it was exactly this kind of male grief that he felt in the wake of his wedding night and everything that followed from it; maybe he wrapped himself in it and kept himself intact there.

Ruskin had asked Hunt not to say anything about his letter to Millais, but Effie "thought it right I should know," as Millais told Hunt, pressing him to go ahead with his journey as "mine is purely a selfish desire to have you in sight." But, he added of Ruskin, "I never saw so strange a person." Hunt did put off his trip until the New Year, and Millais left Glenfinlas two days after the Ruskins, turning up at their hotel in Edinburgh. He was too exhausted to finish the painting this season, he explained—"[Millais] seems quite unsettled by his disappointment with his picture," Ruskin said—but of course what he really needed was to see Effie. And it seems that it was then, or shortly thereafter, that he and she came to an understanding. By spring their feelings for one another were an open secret.

Self-possessed until now, Ruskin began to spin out of control. It was not that he did not understand the situation in his marriage or his own character. He wrote:

> Looking back on myself—I find no change in myself from a boy—from the child except the natural changes wrought by age. I am exactly the same creature—in temper—in likings—

in weaknesses: much wiser—knowing more and thinking more: but in character exactly the same—and so is Effie. When we married, I expected to change *her*—she expected to change *me*. Neither have succeeded, and both are displeased.

He wrote this to his father, of all people, whose pressure on Ruskin to labor and succeed was the analog of Ruskin's mother's overbearing preoccupation with his salvation. Still more dejected, Ruskin began another letter but could not bring himself to post it: "I have hardly any real *warmth* of feeling, except for picture and mountains—I don't want to do anything that I don't; I have no love of gaiety as people call it."

To know this about himself—and all the rest that had been laid bare that summer—was more than Ruskin could stand to know: If that was all he was and it did not signify—in Victorian parlance—what did he amount to? It was enough to feel himself an abyss, and then he found out that Effie intended to divorce him. He was going to lose what he in truth didn't want but would waste and kill himself to hang onto.

His parents marshaled the legal opposition to Effie's divorce suit, which ended in her gynecological examination and, in the end, made public fools of both parents and son. Ruskin himself was deposed to not much effect:

It may be thought strange that I could abstain from a woman who to most people was so attractive. But though her face was beautiful, her person was not formed to excite passion. On the contrary, there were certain circumstances in her person which completely checked it.

Ruskin evaluated Effie as he might have a painting: the technique and conception were commendable, but the whole didn't exceed its parts. It failed at the level of transcendent observation, of truth to nature, as though Effie might have been herself unnatural. It makes no sense to me, nor did it to the court: the divorce would be granted. While they waited for the final decree, Effie and Millais absented themselves from London. Millais returned to Glenfinlas by himself to work on the painting in May:

> Returning to the place is so wonderfully strange that all the rest of what has happened appears a dream. [But] I shall not feel happy until the picture is finished. . . . I almost fancy sometimes that it will never be finished but will last all my life. One thing I dread the thought of is Ruskin sitting to me again for the hands. I have been thinking a great deal of him lately and . . . he is certainly mad.

Ruskin's hands, knitting together in madness: what his hands will be doing in his 1873 self-portrait, chewing the cud of self-abnegation. Millais told Effie's mother just before the divorce was finalized that even the common folk at Glenfinlas could see what Ruskin was like. A woodcutter said that "he was the queerest man he ever saw, and *not like other people* . . . and had *very dull eyes*."

In his next letter Millais wrote, "I am more convinced than ever that J.R. is insane": "I think it very likely that J.R. will go into the church of Rome when his parents die . . . but before long I think he will destroy all doubt in regard to his character by publishing some absurdity which will at once settle the state of mind."

I read this and wonder if Millais is becoming merely self-serving in insisting on Ruskin's insanity. It goes without saying that he'll cancel the final sitting for Ruskin's hands, if only to avoid awkwardness, if not violence: "I shall refuse to paint his hands as there is just a chance mine *perhaps* do what I should afterwards be sorry for."

Millais had already painted the eyes, and they are not dull. They are serene; maybe they are a little like the eyes in *The Light of the World*, if more satisfied, less troubled. Perhaps he, like Jesus, knows something we don't; or maybe it is contained in the hands that Millais finally painted from his preliminary sketches, something that Ruskin's holding onto. But they're not closed. He's

John Everett Millais, *John Ruskin* (1854, oil on canvas). By permission of the Ashmolean Museum, University of Oxford, UK/Bridgeman Images.

holding his hat in one and the other is only slightly cupped, as if something's been released.

The next thing Ruskin published was not the unwitting disclosure of craziness that Millais had predicted but rather a letter to the *Times* about one of the highlights of the new 1854 Royal Academy show. It was a lengthy explication of Hunt's *The Light of the World* that walks the viewer through its iconography, technique, and theoretical basis. He'd been to the gallery the previous day and, being Ruskin, spent not a little time looking at it:

> Standing by it yesterday for upwards of an hour, I watched the effect it produced upon the passers by. Few stopped to look at it, and those who did almost invariably with some contemptuous expression, founded on what appeared to them the absurdity of representing the Saviour with a lantern in his hand.

I would be one of those people and the lantern would be the least of it. And for a moment I imagined Ruskin was going to explain what was wrong with the picture, that he was going to see what I see. But no, he concludes as follows: "I believe there are very few persons on whom the picture, thus justly understood, will not produce a deep impression. For my own part, I think it one of the very noblest works of sacred art ever produced in this or any other age."

I wonder how Ruskin can be so wrong. Not because I am right but because I believe Ruskin is almost never wrong. Either I can't see the greatness in *The Light of the World* or Ruskin was not in his normal rational state: Millais and Effie had driven him mad. Now he swooned before this awful painting by Millais's best friend, humiliated to the point of forsaking his own perfect taste.

A few weeks later, Ruskin was at it again in the pages of the *Times*, again boosting Hunt. Unlike Millais, who was still fiddling with the Glenfinlas portrait—Ruskin's father had made payment in advance—Hunt had finished *The Light of the World* and then tossed off *The Awakening Conscience*, which was just as renowned, controversial, and—to me—awful: maybe not quite as awful, as it doesn't purport to represent the divine, but it has the same unctuously lurid palette, the same constricted vertical composition, and the same disconcerting heads. There's no record of the male model's name, but I could swear it's the same fellow as Christ in *The Light of the World*. As for the woman, here's Ruskin:

I suppose that no one possessing the slightest knowledge of expression could remain untouched by the countenance of the lost girl, rent from its beauty into sudden horror; the lips half open, indistinct in their purple quivering, the teeth set hard, the eyes filled with the fearful light of futurity, and with tears of ancient days.

Myself, I am pretty well untouched, though I see the purple quivering lips. Her sap of a boyfriend/fancy man, for example, looks like she might have plenty of reasons to drop him besides moral epiphany. Then there is the way everything in the room is made to correspond to and mirror everything else: the cat has dragged a dead bird on the rug but has paused before devouring it in order to replicate its mistress's stunned expression. All this, Ruskin thinks, is precisely the point: "There is not a single object in all that room, common, modern, vulgar (in the vulgar sense, as it may be), but it became tragical, if rightly read." And, if rightly read, he concludes "there will not be found one [image] powerful as this to meet full in the front the moral evil of the age in which it is painted, to waken into mercy the cruel thoughtlessness of youth and subdue the severities of judgement into the sanctity of compassion."

I won't—can't—follow Ruskin there. As with *The Awakening Conscience*'s companion piece at the show, the woman's eyes bother me: they're too large, each one bigger than her mouth, and I can't see Ruskin's "fearful light of futurity" in them, still less "tears of ancient days." I am no good about tears, shedding them or detecting them. As with *The Light of the World*'s eyes, I don't know what to make of them. I can't dismiss them, but I also can't quite see them.

But it was only by looking hard at the eyes that I saw the window that is reflected in the mirror behind the woman, which took my breath away. I saw her hair reflected on it, wavy and tumbling down her back rather than pinned up (that's how you know that she and her boyfriend have come to the piano from the bed). Then I saw through the window and beyond it into a cluster of trees in the garden, all of it in sharp focus (like the lighting, the depth of field here is perfectly rendered) and a tonal range of greens in a strong blanching light that only a master of photography could achieve. I'd kill to have made such a picture with my camera.

It's only a window, yet it's the best thing in the painting. It's how, perhaps, men envision a woman: Effie in a window at a Scottish castle; Effie framed vertically or horizontally at her work, reading her book, doing her hair; and Effie at the window at Ruskin's house in the only known defensive account Ruskin gave about their marriage. In a letter a month after the final decree of annulment, he laid down a quick tragicomic sketch of how life was between them:

Effie is looking abstractedly out of the window.
John. "What are looking at, Effie?"
E. "Nothing."
J. "What are you thinking of then?"
E. "A great many things."
J. "Tell me some of them."
E. "I was thinking of operas—and excitement—and—
       (angrily) a great many of things."
J. "And what conclusions did you come to?"
E. "None—because *you* interrupted me."
Dialogue closed.

It's petulant twice over. He's made Effie a pouting child, but you can also hear his own foot stamp furiously as he describes her: *this* is what he's had to put up with. To his credit, it seems to be the only time he truly aimed to make her look bad. Of course, to speak of it cast him in a poor light as either an impotent cuckold or—if he'd connived to set her up with Millais—an impotent pimp: effete, craven, and, as a man, not up to the job.

Ruskin should have been grateful that in short order no one cared. Millais and Effie really did live happily ever after; Millais grew rich and famous, and Effie became the mother of eight and a formidable chatelaine. She continued to be Millais's occasional model, with her perennial expression intact: she remained always nobody's fool.

In the aftermath of the annulment Effie and Millais had nothing more to worry about than the disposition of small matters, such as the images that he made at Glenfinlas: "By the bye what am I to do with the little portrait I did of you with the foxgloves?"

> I have never sent it to [Ruskin], and I know I suppose it is impossible and yet I do not like to keep it after giving it to him—This will appear to you an absurd thing to talk about, but I am so crazed with trying to realize your freedom that I am simply unequal to express myself.

In his next letter he settles his conscience on the matter: "The better way perhaps will be not to say a word about your little portrait to J.R. I am sorry to have to mention his name to you. Poor little Countess what suffering you have gone through."

Ruskin's father paid Millais the balance due on the Glenfinlas portrait in December. In the interim Ruskin had written to Millais, asking if they might remain friends. Millais replied, "I can scarcely see how you conceive it possible that I can desire to continue on terms of intimacy with you." Ruskin accepted Millais's wish but always maintained that he had indeed taught Millais how to paint rocks, plants, and water that summer and had perfected his vision—though it is also true that Millais never, ever painted another landscape portrait.

There is one more thing to say about the aftermath of Ruskin's and Effie's divorce. It takes a while for the full impact of these things to unfold. Certainly that was the case in my own divorce, five years behind me when I went to Glenfinlas. So I'm inclined to think that what happened to Ruskin four years after his divorce might be connected to the events at Glenfinlas and what followed from them.

In the autumn of the previous year and into the winter and spring of 1858, Ruskin had been cataloging and organizing Turner's massive bequest of his work to the British Museum. Among the more than 10,000 drawings were many that Ruskin found "obscene": they were, as he wrote his father, "evidence . . . of a gradual moral decline in the painter's mind." When he alerted the museum authorities to the sketches' presence in the bequest, it was decided that they should be burned. The museum was concerned about the scandal of housing them, Ruskin about their impact on Turner's reputation. More privately, the disillusionment that they produced in Ruskin must have been enormous. Turner had been his greatest hero since he was a teenager and had established him as a critic and a public figure— had made him pretty much entirely what he felt himself to be.

Some of these drawings survive, hidden in sketchbooks that went unnoticed or were only discovered later. They are probably not great art, but neither are they very effective as pornography. They're only sketches: you might say they're suggestive in the benign sense of the word, in the same way that Turner's clouds and water do not so much show as forcefully imply mass and power.

In one sketch, filled out with watercolor, the drawing is entirely perfunctory, except for one thing: the flare of red applied to the vulva, which doesn't evince any obscene anatomical detail but compels the eye to go where, if you are Ruskin, it doesn't care to go. It's easy to formulate what this extraordinary, searing emphasis might say about Turner and, knowing what we know, how it would have struck Ruskin, representing precisely the thing about Effie that he found overwhelming, even disgusting. That Turner, his master, the impetus of his career, rendered it with such a combination of aplomb and force would have appalled him.

Ruskin worked pretty much night and day on the bequest and finished the last of his work on it in May. He needed to recuperate and arranged a three-month journey to the continent alone, free of his parents. In July he arrived in Turin, a city he'd never had much interest in, whose museum featured an artist, Paolo Veronese, whom Ruskin had never much been impressed by. But in viewing Veronese's *The Presentation of the Queen of Sheba to Solomon* Ruskin was enthralled, even transformed. He saw something in it beyond his previous ken and stayed six weeks to sketch and study it: "I merely think that Paul Veronese was ordained by Almighty God to be an archangel." It was the sumptuousness and majesty of the painting—its panoply of dogs, doves, lions, Africans, beauties, maids and hangers-on, and gilded splendors—that seized him, but also its humor, its sly hidden jests, and, most of all, its celebration of the human body as the apex of created beauty.

This had not been Ruskin's aesthetic or, for that matter, his theology up to now: following Turner's lead, he had focused on mountains, rocks, water, weather, and all their particularities—the divine manifest in nature. But perhaps he'd lost his faith in Turner and put Veronese, sublime but also humane, in his place.

> Is this mighty Paul Veronese, in whose soul there is a strength as of the snowy mountains, and within whose brain all the pomp and majesty of humanity floats in a marshalled glory, capacious and serene like clouds at sunset—this man whose finger is as fire, and whose eye is like the morning—is he a servant of the devil; and is the poor little wretch in a tidy black tie, to whom I have been listening this Sunday morning expounding Nothing with a twang—is he a servant of God?

Ruskin had been in broad sympathy with the romantic animism of Emerson and his ilk, but now he became even more deeply convinced that art and the divine were inextricably bound—that art communicated the divine more completely and deeply than religion, could perhaps even replace it:

> Has God made faces beautiful and limbs strong, and created these strange, fiery, fantastic energies, and created the splen-

dour of substance and the love of it; created gold, and pearls, and crystal, and the sun that makes them gorgeous; and filled human fancy with all splendid thoughts; and given to the human touch its power of placing and brightening and perfecting, only that all these things may lead His creatures away from Him?

From that day forward, Ruskin was "a conclusively *un*-converted man"; "my evangelical beliefs were put away." And with that, his artistic interests began to change: he was less preoccupied with the geological and natural forms he saw at Glenfinlas than with the human body, "the highest visible work of God." His language would always remain charged with Christian imagery, vocabulary, and history—but his idea of the divine would become unorthodox and more Emersonian, more convinced that the divine was most present in the visible world and in the body in particular.

Those epiphanies seem to be present in one of the most beautiful, compassionate, and disturbing things Ruskin ever wrote, a recollection of another sight from that same stay in Turin:

A girl of ten or twelve, it might be: one of the children to whom there has never been any other lesson taught than that of patience;—patience of famine and thirst; patience of heat and cold; patience of fierce word and sullen blow; patience of changeless fate and giftless time. She was lying with her arms thrown back over her head, all languid and lax, on an earth-heap by the river side (the softness of dust being the only softness she had ever known), in the southern suburb of Turin, one golden afternoon, years ago. She had been at her play, after her fashion, with other patient children, and had thrown herself down, full in the sun, like a lizard. The sand was mixed with the draggled locks of her black hair, and some of it sprinkled over her face and body, in an "ashes to ashes" sort of way; a few black rags about her loins, but her limbs nearly bare, and her little breasts, scarce dimpled yet, —white, —marble-like—but, as wasted marble, thin with scorching and the reins of time. So she lay, motionless: black and white by the shore in the sun; the yellow light flickering back on her from the passing eddies of the river, and burning down on her from the west.

It's an exquisite piece of description that reveals Ruskin's emerging sense of social justice, but we can also see the direction in which his desire is moving, his notion of which bodies are beautiful and which ones are erotic for him; what a woman—or a girl—might be to him, after Effie.

Millais had already painted Emily Patmore in the same year that he finished Ruskin's portrait and Hunt exhibited *The Light of the World*, when her husband, Coventry, published *The Angel in the House.* Everyone knew the Angel was based on Emily. Shortly after publication she died the death of an angelic girl from consumption, a "wasting disease," a sort of counter-anorexia, which might have come from having given altogether too much of herself. There was something of the child in the ideal of womanhood that Patmore created, a hybrid of virginality and self-sacrifice, both devoted and devout. Virginia Woolf described it as follows:

She was intensely sympathetic. She was immensely charming. She was utterly unselfish. She excelled in the difficult arts of family life. She sacrificed herself daily. If there was chicken, she took the leg; if there was a draught she sat in it—in short she was so constituted that she never had a mind or a wish of her own, but preferred to sympathize always with the minds and wishes of others. Above all—I need not say it—she was pure. Her purity was supposed to be her chief beauty—her blushes, her great grace.

That's better than I could ever put it. But I also think that the Angel represented a middle way between even less palatable avenues by which middle- and upper-class Victorian men approached women.

On the one hand, there's the virgin/whore dichotomy exemplified by the novelists Wilkie Collins and George Gissing: neither could quite bring himself to fuck—that seems the best word—a woman of his own class; truly, unashamedly, joyfully fuck, even—and perhaps especially—in marriage. So they took mistresses from the lower orders, or in Collins's case established what amounted to a secret marriage with one, with house and children. But I am not sure, reading them and their biographies, that the virgin/whore model quite describes their situation: it seems less that women of their own class—whom they could respectably marry—were too pure, too ideal, to touch than that they were confounding, even intimidating.

On the other hand, there's pedophilia as practiced by Lewis Carroll and many others, which today discomfits pretty much anyone: chaste pedophilia defying both our logic and what we think we know about human nature in the same way Ruskin's virginity does. We cannot imagine *not* sexualizing an object of desire. Maybe this is one of chief differences between the Victorians and us: not that they were repressed and we are not, but that for them gender is pretty much insurmountable unless it can be tamed in the manner of *The Angel in the House*. It was terrifying in the way that the artistic sublime was: at once both awful (in the literal sense) and uplifting, mystical.

Ruskin ended up at the pedophile end of this spectrum, but unlike Carroll, for whom girls were above all sweet, Ruskin's desire was steeped in the paranoid sublime. Shortly after returning from Turin, he fell in love with an Anglo-Irish girl named Rose La Touche. She was nine and he was thirty-nine. He was obsessed with her for the rest of his life.

Ruskin drew Rose's portrait in 1862 when she was twelve, and it is nothing like his 1850 sketch of Effie: it is grounded, fully detailed, and—against expectation—Rose is as much a woman as she is a girl; she's lovely yet has serious things on her mind. In a self-portrait of Ruskin made at about the same time, he looks sharp as a tack and quite handsome. And the eyes are how we imagine Ruskin's ideal of eyes ought to look: inquiring, confident without being smug; he sees you and everything else, and that's the core of his desire.

But eleven years later Ruskin will draw his tormented self-portrait in the blue scarf. In 1863 he believed he'd reached an understanding with Rose's parents that he and Rose would be betrothed when she came of age in 1867. But she refused him, ostensibly on the grounds that he had lost the evangelical faith that was so central to her life. But that loss arguably constituted the main business of his becoming his own man, the one with the comprehending near-omniscient gaze—except in the matter of women, knowing what he and they might be to each other; what they might, as with Effie at the window, have to say to one another.

Ruskin went mad instead. He obsessed about Rose at first and then began hallucinating about her, mainly as St. Ursula, a Christian princess who refused to marry a pagan king, which is more or less how she and her parents construed the agnostic Ruskin. Thereafter, he went deeper and deeper into paranoia and manic ecstasies, painting Rose asleep in the manner of St. Ursula. He was still visited by almost every eminence of the current day, including Lewis Carroll, who photographed him not at ease but seemingly lucid, ever watchful. Coventry Patmore, too, came to the Lake District. He and Carroll might have told Ruskin a great deal, though not enough for him to make sense of Rose or Effie and still less of himself or Millais's uncanny trick of turning longing into happiness.

I went to Scotland, not of course in 1853, but that was the idea: to immerse myself in a simulacrum of it. I brought my camera and wanted to photograph the spot in the Glen where the three of them had stood or sat and painted, read, and stared downriver. I wanted to make it look a little like Hunt's window if I could.

I hadn't done much photography since college; really, since I was a teenager. But photographing these places seemed like a way into them that might take me beyond whatever I could think and say about them. I was going to do it with traditional film and darkroom photographic paper, not to re-create something closer to Victorian photographic conditions but to make the process slower, more considered, more difficult. That last desire might be a pretense, but I also believed that a straight negative, untouched by anything other than the light of the place, would be truer, more real, than a digital image processed and primped on a computer—that Ruskin's gneiss photographed in analog mode would be akin to his drawing of it.

I began at Doune Castle, where the Ruskins and Millais stopped on the way to Glenfinlas and Millais conceived the idea to paint Effie at the window as a companion to the Ruskin portrait. The castle was not in ruins, or no more ruined than in 1853, the exterior walls more intact than the interior. Among the few inside windows, I found just two where Millais could have placed Effie for a portrait, so I set up my tripod—it was quite dark inside and the exposure would have to be long—and focused on those. There was light and there was tan stone and not much else to see, except shadows, and those fell oblong or pooled, not black but brown, a darker shade than the stone, more a tint than a color.

To reach the first window, Effie would have had to climb a few steps—less steps, really, than rough-cut blocks cemented into place—to a small ledge on the right where she could stand. The light would have fallen entirely on the left side of her face; it would not, for that reason alone, have been a cheery portrait: it would not be sly Effie but inscrutable Effie or pensive Effie, or maybe she would be content but not too obviously happy. That's the way to be in a castle, with someone who might be falling in love looking up at you from a few feet below, deciding where the highlights fall most beautifully upon your face.

My highlights fell on the wall, chiefly in a lozenge-shaped patch just behind where Effie might have stood (the light pretty much at the same angle because it was almost exactly the same time of year), which would mean that Effie's body would have blocked it: the light—such as it was—would have been entirely hers. The second window was better lit: she could have stood at its center in the posture of the figure in Millais's *Mariana* of 1851, the year he met the Ruskins.

Mariana is a character from Shakespeare's *Measure for Measure* adapted by Tennyson: "When thickest dark did trance the sky, She drew her casement-curtain by, and glanced athwart the glooming flats," waiting for her lover to come in sight, knowing that he never will, having abandoned her when her dowry was lost in a shipwreck.

Mariana had Effie's hair and something like her nose, though that's a coincidence since Millais had scarcely met her at this point. The pose, according to some art historians, is meant to show her stretching as she stands up from a long spell at her needlework while keeping an eye on the window. But I don't see it that way: she seems too relaxed, too self-contained, like a cat rising from a nap. And I can't help but notice her out-thrust breasts and her hands at her back that seem to be pushing her hips forward, as though she's displaying her sexual beauty—her desire and desirability—maybe even offering it to no one in particular, but just to the window that frames her from the outside. Millais probably wouldn't have consciously painted with that in mind, at least not before he'd met Mrs. Ruskin.

I wanted to imagine it that way: Effie presenting herself at the window, but the window was empty, and I was a good distance from it since I was using a long lens. That placed me in the way of other visitors, who were good-natured about the inconvenience that I'd created. Maybe I was spoiling the atmosphere (medieval, bloody, bloody-minded) with my tripod and the camera's slap and thump as the shutter fired, but they were politely cautious about crossing in front of me and blocking my view. I told them not to worry; that the shots would take a long time to set up because (I didn't say this) I didn't know what I was doing; technically, for sure, but also in some other way having to do with intention or conviction that it ought to be done at all.

I left with relief: the experience, which was supposed to be precisely that—an *experience*—felt slight. I hadn't really communed with anyone, but then Millais hadn't made the painting he intended to do here, though he'd written to Hunt that he "never saw anything so beautiful." Ruskin reported to his father that Millais had "been more struck by the castle of Doune than anything and is determined to paint Effie at one of its windows." He wrote that from Glenfinlas, where events were perhaps already moving swiftly; where Effie looked more beautiful than any castle; where the midges were biting and the trail was shoe-sucking mud; where painting was not supposed to be an ordeal but a lark.

I slept that night in a country hotel—a very nicely done-up farmhouse with great food—between Doune and Glenfinlas. They upgraded my room and fed me Angus beef raised on the property. On top of that, the girl, nineteen or so, at the front desk enchanted me. She had an intense but not indecipherable accent and said "wee" for "small" with no self-consciousness. She and her colleagues were feeling their Scottish oats: the Scottish National Party had captured every seat north of the border in the British national election the day before, overturning the status quo to such a degree that it seemed both the ruling Conservative and opposition Labour parties would be in Scotland's thrall.

It had snowed, she told me, a few days before, but now the sun was out. In the morning I looked out onto an enormous field that extended to a range of hills with a single bull standing in it. It might have been autumn, though it was the end of May.

I ate breakfast and told the girl at the desk how good the housemade marmalade had been. I thought, wouldn't it be fun to call her Effie, just for myself, in my mind. I loaded my camera gear into the car and drove a long time along the narrow road parallel to the lake. The sky was mottled with clouds and intermittent sun-breaks, but mostly a continuous gray that ran from charcoal to pewter. I'd planned for rain and mud—for the conditions of 1853—and brought a pair of rubber Wellington boots, a slicker, and a transparent waterproof sleeve for the camera. Against the midges, I had only hope.

I got to Brig O'Turk in forty-five minutes. There was a pub and tea-shop on the site of the hotel where the Ruskins and Millais stayed for a few nights. Judging by the number of cars parked in front, it was doing a good business. Three hundred yards up the road was the schoolmaster's cottage that they'd rented for the remainder of the summer, white with bright blue doors. I parked just beyond it where the road was gated and walked up toward Glenfinlas dam, under whose reservoir the site of Millais's painting had long been supposed to be submerged. But in August 1993 it was rediscovered by the art historian Alistair Grieve downstream of the dam. The water level, vegetation, and geology were reportedly identical to those of 140 years before.

There was supposed to be a newly installed sign pointing out the spot, though I couldn't see one anywhere. I wasn't sure how I'd find the site on my own: the woods between the road and the river that I could hear below were thick with spindly trees and the banks looked inhospitably steep.

But in another hundred yards the road curved to the right, and in its left-hand bow I saw a fenced clearing with a wooden marker perhaps four feet high that said this was the place. Twenty-five feet below, the water roared and seethed. The bank was forty-five degrees—steeper in places—with no obvious steps or footholds and only roots to hang onto. How I would do it with a camera and tripod I couldn't imagine, still less how the Ruskins and Millais did it in Victorian dress plus easel and paints.

Months later, I'd learn that there was a gentler path upstream but now I clambered down, feet slipping beneath me on the slick mud, clinging to roots I wasn't sure would hold me. I wondered how or if I would get back up the bank. But I was on a quest—a grandiose one—and I was up against my cowardice, my laziness, and what seemed like my life-long incapacity to amount to something.

It seemed a long time before my feet touched level ground. It was sharp-edged rock, Ruskin's gneiss, unworn, almost untouched by the abrasion of water. What struck me most, though, was the coloration of the place, the palette and cast of the whole scene exactly that of Millais's portrait—an umber ground with muted green highlights, which in contradiction to the laws of color added up to something like rust, something like oxblood. The place might well be dark if it weren't for the turbid white stream cutting through it.

The water was higher than in Millais's painting or sketches—a product of the recent snow and rainfall I'd heard mentioned—but I quickly saw the rock on which Ruskin stood, angled up like a ship's prow; the level area to its left where Effie read and sketched; Millais's place downstream from them both; and, across the stream from Ruskin's perch, the gneiss formation.

I set up my camera on the tripod and tried to photograph each of these spots in both color and black-and-white, swapping the film back with each shot. My feet weren't steady—the rock was too slick—and neither was the tripod. I feared the camera would fall into the river; still more, that I would. I think my hands shook. I dropped a film holder, which bounced and dented. I was anxious; in truth I was afraid. This was Ruskin's sublime: it was scary, not bucolic or romantic—none of the things it was for the three of them—but menacing. I forced myself to take the pictures that I thought I needed to take and climbed the bank—butt and knees smeared with mud—to safety.

Back above and secure within the perimeter of the fence, I sat down on a boulder to change film. I grabbed another roll from my bag and loaded it into the camera. What I failed to notice, however, was that the new roll had already been exposed and contained my closest, sharpest images of the gneiss formation. It should have been next to impossible (with warnings all over the backing paper), but I'd been lost in my thoughts. When I tried to wind the film forward I realized that something was wrong, but it took me several more minutes to figure out what it was. The camera was jammed and, worse, the exposed roll that I had put in wouldn't come out. I applied force that for all I knew might break the camera. But I'd come a long way to photograph this place: if the camera were annihilated in the process that would be one more part of the story.

But what story was that? From my spot beside the fence, I could look down and visualize Ruskin, Effie, and Millais arranged in a triangle, day after day all through that summer: Ruskin upstream at one vertex, Millais downstream, and beautiful Effie midway between them to his left at the other, close to the bank I'd just climbed, reading Dante aloud over the roar. Nothing had changed, not so much as a single stone. They could have been there, not just in my mind's eye but independent of it: Ruskin's acute observing oblivion as he gazes downstream: Millais painting distractedly because he's stealing glances at Effie; Effie knowing she has two men or, rather, nothing to her right and something to her left. They begin to leave when the light begins to fail: Ruskin first, as is his wont, to go back to writing his lecture in the cottage; then, a little later, Effie and Millais. At some point along the bank or the rutted path, one of them slips and falls and it's then that they kiss—or, really, that she kisses him.

I had finally been able to unjam the camera, load my last roll of film, and take some shots from above the river. There wasn't much light, so I had to use a low shutter speed, which made the water blur. That, I think now, is how it should be. Because I slowed down the water, just as Millais had, who slowed it, of course, to a standstill. The blurring is a photographic cliché, I guess, but with no digital manipulation, no colors that "pop" or roiling Photoshop contrasts. So it was what the camera "saw," naked and true to nature, as Ruskin would have had it, and it's what I saw too, or have come to see, holding the print in my hands, the one real thing.

But I sensed that Annie, the art historian with whom I'd argued about the Pre-Raphaelites, might have been right: nothing in artistic terms was really advanced here. The blurred water in my photographs wasn't running downstream but running backward. Maybe the venture I'd undertaken was all regress, not progress. It had thrown me backward, deeper into the confusions of time;

the welter of ungraspable things that we would have to do to see it clearly. That, I think, was what I had aimed at in coming to Glenfinlas, where I imagined I'd recover something and preserve it in my photographs. It was a fool's errand, too clever by half in assuming that I could marshal what I thought of as art to accomplish it.

That's because art has its own devices and intentions. A few months later, I quoted the line "poetry makes nothing happen" to a friend who knows his W. H. Auden. I was being glib and ironic. I might have meant it or might not: our art—anybody's art—might amount to no more than gestures or, by chance, might contain something necessary and true. But my friend brought me up short: the line meant, he explained, that art and poetry do make *nothing* happen literally, in a substantial sense: unveil what's unseen to the unaided, un-Ruskinian eye, make what's absent present. It can't be summoned on command; the art-making comes from waiting, from attention. It might take a whole summer and some of the following spring, long enough that you might fall in love, the painting might end up revealing what you did and didn't see, the man in the river and the longing accreting along the bank, just out of sight.

Later—actually, a few days before I wrote this—I found another Millais drawing of Effie online. It's dated 1852, but I know that's wrong. It's clearly from the summer of 1853. There were a few brief occasions during which he might have drawn her the previous year, but not as he does here. She has put on the best dress she brought to the cottage and is posing in front of a mirror. In fact, she's curtseying before it, paying homage to her own image, a hint of erotic grace contained in the way her dress is falling off her shoulder. Millais, of course, saw all this—probably saw much more given his emotional state—but he saw it as a bystander. Effie might have been amusing herself in a display of real or mock vanity, reverting to girlish dress-up, practicing how to be a lady.

Or maybe it was a bit of playacting that she and Millais concocted to pass the time as Ruskin wrote his lectures and the rain hammered down outside: when we are grown-ups together, you and I, this is how we'll be, how I'll look, how you'll see me.

When I got back to the hotel, it had begun to rain, and as I unloaded the car—my boots, my tripod, a heap of Sunday newspapers that I hadn't got around to reading—it was pouring. I trudged into the reception room and said hello to the girl: red-haired, I saw now, amused but not haughty, my Effie. I was aiming to chit-chat with her, just shy of flirtation—I imagined that she might have had it in her to return the favor. But I stood there, dripping onto the slate floor as if paralyzed and struck dumb. Had it been a good day, she asked? Oh, lovely, I said; an adventure, too, and indicated my muddy jeans. She laughed, and it seemed to me in the instant that we'd had a moment, reached an understanding.

In the morning, she was at the desk when I checked out. After she'd returned my credit card, she reached under the desk and set a crock of marmalade before me. We thought you'd like this, she said. I thanked her profusely, maybe tenderly, as though she'd said *I* thought you'd like this, which is how I took it in spite of the facts, the way I wanted it to be.

Back in London, I wished I could see Annie, the art historian I'd dated. I'd tell her she was right about Ruskin and the whole Pre-Raphaelite bunch, to say nothing of Hunt and his Jesus, whose eyes promised nothing but more uncertainty, as incomprehensible as Effie's eyes were to Ruskin. But I didn't try to reach her: as she'd said, I had evaded important truths with her. God, too, must like to be elusive, likes to withhold himself, likes to make us feel he's out of reach, plays to our knack for thinking it's all our fault. The Victorians, whose doubt teetered in perfect balance with faith, knew this. Hunt gave them the Jesus they wanted, the one that Ruskin, in spite of himself, came to know was impossible.

As I write this, it's the end of summer 164 years later, and the three of them might still be at it, things unfolding, the easel set up on the rocks, the midges biting, eyes stealing glances, eyes lost in thought, blind to some things, making too much of others. The other day I found one last Millais drawing, and it settles one of my questions.

It's a sketch of Effie at Doune Castle—not so much a sketch as a doodle on a page with other random images surrounding it. You can see she's standing at the second window—the window where Mariana is offering her body, as I'd conceived it—and, as Millais planned, Effie's hat is on the ledge.

The page is half in Scotland—Effie, the castle, a lamb—and half in Renaissance Italy. Millais had a style for both: a fine, tentative line for Effie and a heavier, rounder cartoonish one for the bearded classically headed man and the putto to the other side of him. And when you turn the page, there's more of the same. They're all a little ridiculous: Mary tending the hair of a pensive, day-dreaming Jesus; lumpy workers in pantaloons; and a lachrymose, spindly-fingered male clutching a crucifix and gazing plangently toward heaven, St. Peter perhaps.

These latter figures are puffed-up, exaggerated caricatures. Millais is having fun with them, whereas with Effie at the window he's being straightforward. I can't say he's in love with her yet, but he's trying to capture the scene, not characterize it. He's also in full artistic sympathy with Ruskin because what he's cartooning—mocking—on the rest of the page and on its reverse is art in the post-Raphaelite mode, begot by Raphael and the mannerists descended from him, who, in Ruskin's formulation, "rendered finish of execution and beauty of form the chief objects of all artists; and henceforward execution was looked for rather than thought, and beauty rather than veracity." And Millais had come to Scotland to learn veracity.

I had too, not quite knowing it. I had been laboring under a kind of refusal to see things as they are—in particular, love and the kind of people I might love; the kind of people who might love me. In love, the novelist Stendhal said, everything signifies, is prophecy or legend: everything past and future, every cause and effect, leads back to the eternal now of the love story—to, really, the novel(ty?) of it. It will have a denouement and, unless you learn to differentiate between novels and life—learn to go beyond "finish of execution and beauty of form"—as often as not it will be tragic. Sad to say, there's more truth in an outcropping of gneiss than in any such love story you might pick up; more truth, you might think, even in Hunt's Christ with his lantern and inscrutable eyes, in which you can make out no more than baffling actuality.

Chapter 2

I HELD IT in reserve for a rainy day, illness, or maybe despair. I had read every Dickens novel except one: *Our Mutual Friend*, the last one he finished. The idea of running out, of exhausting the canon, distressed me, so I kept it as though behind glass to be removed in case of emergency or catastrophe; in case I sensed that my own canon—my desire to make it, to live it—was guttering out.

I didn't, in fact, wait until any of those things happened; I read it when the thought came to me, half-whimsical, half-haunted, that fate might arrange things differently than I'd planned and I might never get to read it at all. Then I read it again a year later and then again (because I couldn't get enough of it) on the 150th anniversary of its publication in serial form in 1864 and 1865. I read an installment of it each month via online facsimiles of the pamphlet-sized magazines as Dickens issued it, sandwiched between pages of advertisements for the essentials and ephemera of Victorian life: corsets, bustles, mustard, patent medicines, silverware, fainting couches, and other people's novels in triple-decker format, in two-shilling budget editions, and matched deluxe sets of the author's complete works: Elizabeth Gaskell, George Eliot, Wilkie Collins, William Thackeray, Anthony Trollope, and, of course, Charles Dickens himself.

Dickens was a canny businessman. By the time he began *Our Mutual Friend* he was immensely rich, as rich as any writer had ever been; rich enough to buy the mansion he coveted as a child and set up his wife in her own Regent's Park house, having cast her off for a young actress. He knew about money and what could be done with it, what it could do for and to people.

Our Mutual Friend is a novel about money, but you could say all of Dickens is about money or, more exactly, being poor or in debt and then, usually by happenstance, coming into money, usually a great deal of it, enough to launch the beneficiary into a higher class. It's that much better if the money is the result of virtue; if it comes from a kind and unknown benefactor or, conversely, is appropriated by luck from a spendthrift or a miser. Often Dickens heroes enjoy it in moderation—learn not to let it spoil them—or renounce it altogether in favor of an even worthier beneficiary.

I have been a beneficiary; on a small scale when I was younger and on a larger scale as I've gotten older, as my elders died off and their wills were read: at first $20,000 a year and more recently nearly $100,000. I'm not rich, but I can live very comfortably on the proceeds; I can write what I want without much interruption beyond the teaching I like to do; I can write things like this book without care. I worry about what I say, how I say it, and whether it will attract some readers, but not much about getting paid.

People doubtless envy me this. I think some of them dismiss what I write altogether because of it; because the writing comes at too low a cost, not as a vocation but as a hobby I could indulge in while other writers do hackwork and pull espressos and teach freshman composition. I did hackwork too once upon a time—press releases, ghostwriting, advertorials, and corporate newsletters—but I've almost forgotten all that. I've become a creature of my comforts.

So you may conclude that what I say here isn't truly "earned"— one of those catchphrases used in writing workshops—and, no, I suppose it's not. It seems to me that I labor hard over it, but it's just a slice of my life you're invited to stumble through alongside me, not unlike reality television, the inconsequential troubles of the comfortably off. There is some suffering but also the kind of comeuppance that people with easy money deserve when they don't renounce it or learn to use it well.

Myself, I seem to be without misgivings; when I read Dickens I root for his people to come into money—to realize "expectations"—as much as I do for them to find lost friends and relatives or to fall in love and marry. I like to see misers come undone, not only because they don't share and have a hoary, unattractive compulsion but because they don't enjoy their money. They should travel in business class and drop $100 on a bottle of wine when they get the chance. I would.

Dickens's father was a colossal debtor who maintained a blithe and probably calculated posture of innocence about the money he was always losing or not repaying. The cause was always bad luck or misunderstanding or someone else's malfeasance, which was meant to excuse his absence from his family in debtor's prison as well as the necessity to send Dickens to work in a blacking factory at the age of twelve. That didn't make Dickens avaricious or, when he got some money, a spendthrift or a miser. But it let him see that money cuts both ways: it takes away as much as it gives and it's never free, especially when it's a gift.

I know something of that too or ought to. The main reason for my own good fortune is my father, specifically his death when I was seven. The money that would have gone to him on his own father's death passed to me. Had he lived a full life, I'd doubtless still be waiting to come into it, given how long-lived our family is.

As things have ended up, I should be grateful for my circumstances, which were the reverse of the situation of Dickens, who was impoverished by his father, not enriched; who was ashamed of his father; whose business in life was to compensate for his father's failings. My own father was liked and admired, athletic and enterprising, someone whom I could have taken pride in; someone who could have taken pride in me.

But he had, I suppose, no choice but to leave my mother—or it must have seemed that way to him. When they separated, he moved away and then got sick and died. I was three when he left. If I did not feel abandoned thereafter, I felt unmoored; there was a gap, a large one, that I sensed but could not quite identify. I knew that our family was not like other families: someone was absent and on that account we were odd, maybe off-putting or repellent to others. Someone was away, not in debtor's prison, but irretrievably removed to some other place. I wasn't ashamed of him—how could I be?: what, after all, had he ever done to me? But I was, for insistent reasons whose logic evaded me, ashamed of myself. That's the way children are: with a limited sense of where others leave off and they begin, they can easily believe that they cause things to happen when those things cannot otherwise be explained. So I felt besmirched, marked out, spoiled, not in the sense of being indulged but in the sense of being ruined, soiled, decomposed.

The other kind of spoiling would come later. My mother and other adults would try to compensate for what I didn't have by giving me what I wanted; things, of course, but also a nearly unrestricted license to do whatever I pleased, a world undelimited by the word "no." Anything else would seem catastrophic to me, something like imprisonment or suffocation, worse than death. I couldn't imagine what death might be, but it might be like that, the everlasting No. Or maybe I didn't really want to know about death, sensing that if I did I might find myself complicit in my father's; that the autonomy I wanted could satisfy both what I wished for and what I wished away. It was contingent upon the absence of a father, whose customary role is to be the giver of rules, the avatar of No.

I wouldn't want to press the comparison—converse rather than truly parallel—too far. I wasn't sent to Dickens's blacking factory; I never went without a meal or shoes. I have a friend who also lost her father when she was a child and inherited his money, and she feels guilty about this unearned boon. She's thrifty almost to a fault: she believes, I think, that the money can't touch her if it isn't spent. She's conscious of the freedom from labor that it affords her but feels that she has to work as hard or harder than anyone else to justify herself. In her own mind, her inherited worth has come at the expense of her own worth.

I came up with an idea and was proud of its ingenuity. Why not, I suggested, think of her inheritance as compensation, as redress for the death of her father; for everything she lost by not having him in her life? Her trust fund was paltry in comparison to what had been taken from her. She should enjoy what it could buy: let it be reparation for the suffering she inherited alongside it, both her fortune and her misfortune.

After we talked, as I walked home—like Dickens, I have a cheerful, untiring itch to walk in the city, mile after mile—it occurred to me that I'd never applied this prescription to my own life and that I ought to. Because I was in my own way as troubled as she was. In my case, I made the money go away not by thrift but by burning through it, by not saving a penny of it. Either way—mine or hers—it disappeared, or so we pretended. And I thought how clever my suggestion was—then, not much more than a minute later, that it rang false: that it meant taking on another sense of entitlement that felt just as unearned as the money did. It felt less like recompense than like revenge, and maybe the revenge's object was the fathers we had lost. We had made them pay. What I'd actually done for my friend was to insult her, cheapening her predicament by monetizing it. Money is perplexing and uncanny in that way: it enriches and degrades, exalts and shames.

Dickens understood that. *Our Mutual Friend* is his final word on the subject, his magnum opus on his greatest preoccupation, his *Das Kapital*. He understood something of what his contemporary

Marx did, but he was also a Freudian in advance of Freud. By the time he came to write *Our Mutual Friend* he understood that money equates to nothing so much as shit: to how shit is hoarded and excreted, how it perfumes and stinks. The controlling images of the novel are the polluted, corpse-laden Thames and the dust mounds near King's Cross, the sewer and the garbage dump. Ranged against these are love, hope, and blind luck. It seems to me an uneven contest, unfair and unwarranted, simultaneously rigged and random.

As I said, I doubt that anyone feels for me: my dilemma still leaves me crying all the way to the bank. Whether or not other people in fact envy me, I've envied myself. Money induces narcissism among other things, and I'm capable of looking in the mirror and thinking, "What a lucky guy." Against all other kinds of feeling, having money surely feels best. Yet, looking in the mirror, I am strangely unsure I am that guy at all.

My usual modus operandi in consuming Dickens is to read him in bed, especially when I'm ill. Maybe illness is the one thing I can convince myself I'm unreservedly entitled to. There are a lot of hypochondriacs among heirs and beneficiaries, but when I'm sick I feel justified as I rarely otherwise do: alive, happily ordinary, paying my dues in a universal human currency of suffering. Swaddled under the covers and a little feverish, I'm swaddled yet again by the novel, by its warmth, humor, and faith that all will be well, that things will turn out in the end, by the 800th or 900th page.

What possessed me to give up the pleasure of my bed I cannot say, but I read *Our Mutual Friend* on my sofa. I was leaving for England soon. I meant to dig into the novel's provenance there, to walk its imaginary streets in a kind of anachronistic stupor, staring at rooflines and doorways while everyone else—real people living in the real world—went about the business of coming and going, getting and spending. When I do this, I suppose I must seem to gawk and stare, which makes me nervous, as though I'm going to be caught and taken to task, sent on my way, or at least laughed at. When I get my camera out and put it on the tripod, the voyeurism is that much more blatant. People cotton on to me. Once when I was photographing a junk shop in Hackney, the owner came out and shouted, "If you wasn't across the street, I'd have the law on you." He knew that as long as I didn't step onto his property I was scot free—but he didn't like his place being gawped at, being made into an object of my longing, my idiot gaze.

That was the only time this ever happened—people don't care or, more likely, don't notice: I'm a ghost photographing ghosts—but it unnerved me. I had a sense of an impending catastrophe or one narrowly averted. I'd been trying to extract the past out of the present: maybe this is unwise, a risky business, a piece of hubris. Nothing good can come of it. So while some people ignore me or laugh at my folly, a few—the tetchy junk dealer—try to warn me before I bring the roof down on my head. When I developed the photo I'd made of his place, I saw that it was badly overexposed, whited out by altogether too much light, too much blind intention.

Dickens's initial, intuitive inspiration for *Our Mutual Friend* seems to have come from noticing a bill posted in Limehouse, the East End's squalid riverside district, which he recorded in his journal: " 'Found Drowned.' The descriptive bill upon the wall, by the waterside—A 'long shore' man—woman—child—or family. Query—connect the Found Drowned Bill with this?" Then, later in the journal, he wrote: "LEADING INCIDENT FOR A STORY. A man—young and eccentric?—feigns to be dead and is dead to all intents and purposes external to himself, and for years retains that singular view of life and character."

And now Dickens had it. Add only the dramas of love and money. He'd extract both from the river and from the dust mounds: the hero will fake his death in the river; the unbeknownst "expecta-tions" that he is meant to inherit will come from the fortune of the owner of the mounds. With the heir presumed dead, the money goes to the kindly, avuncular caretaker of the mounds—he's known as "the Golden Dustman" thereafter—who may be morally and psychologically ruined by it. Love will come when the hero is hired by the Golden Dustman as his private secretary and meets the spoiled, haughty girl that his boss has taken in to give her the advantages of wealth, the pointedly named Bella.

It's a preposterous plot, of course, even by Dickens standards. We tolerate it—the unbelievable characters and situations that fly in the face of the rules of present-day fiction—because his mode and intention are ultimately comic and all the parts move toward reconciliation, marriage, and good fortune. The tragic (which is perhaps only another term for realistic), with its inexorable, irreversible losses and tears, isn't allowed in the door for too long. The good become very good indeed, and the bad are proved to be not so very bad after all.

But as I read, I was not sure that was the case with *Our Mutual Friend*. I sensed that the novel was of two minds, at least about money: that money would drag people down, suck them under the water as Dickens's dominant image would have it; that the cheerful, generous dustman would become a spiteful miser; that Bella (egged on by the dustman, who tells her "Those good looks of yours are worth money") would become ever more vain and avaricious, calculating an advantageous marriage as she might calculate the price of jewelry; that romantic love would descend into envious, violent mania.

The novel averts all these ends but, to me, not very convincingly. It's as though at the last minute the ship avoids the rocks, although the rudder has in fact remained jammed, its true course the same one it set sail on from the start. Dickens brings in a *deus ex machina*, but a god without a face or a name: not even mere good fortune, because the novel Dickens began and never fully departed from does not really believe in good fortune. It believes in the inexorability of drownings, being buried in shit, in disaster. From nearly the beginning this is its world: "The white face of the winter day came sluggishly on, veiled in a frosty mist; and the shadowy ships in the river slowly changed to black substances; and the sun, blood-red on the eastern marshes behind dark masts and yards, seemed filled with the forest it had set on fire." In sum, as Dickens puts it, the locale of *Our Mutual Friend* is no more or less than "the great black river . . . stretching away to the great ocean, Death."

Then there's Jenny Wren. She is one of Dickens's eccentrics, the people who work in professions you didn't know existed, selling the world's detritus out of dusty shop fronts: forgotten documents and sheaths of papers, taxidermy, outdated, useless household junk, and ship's chandlery, stuff that somehow escaped the dust mound. In *Our Mutual Friend*, for example, a shop trades in bones and preserved body parts scavenged and sold by a character named Mr. Venus, whose name suggests that he might be dealing in romance rather than the flotsam of death. In his own estimation, he's an aesthete—people fail to "appreciate the art of my business"—not a ghoul: a purveyor of a counter-beauty, but beauty all the same.

Jenny Wren, who earns her keep sewing doll's dresses, is a crone in a child's body who, though twelve or so, refers to her "old bones." She calls her alcoholic father "bad child," as if she, not he, were the parent. Nor, she says, are her friends like other children's playmates:

> "For when I was a little child," in a tone as though it were ages ago, "the children that I used to see early in the morning were very different than any others that I ever saw. They were not like me: they were not chilled, anxious, ragged, or beaten. . . . All in white dresses . . . they used to come down in long bright slanting rows, and say all together, 'Who is this in pain? Who is this in pain?' . . . And I used to cry out, 'Oh, my blessed children, it's poor me! Have pity on me! Take me up and make me light!' "

Victorian attitudes about children are said to be sentimental, and plenty of orphans, street urchins, and Little Nells die brave deaths. But Jenny Wren is something else: Dickens writes her as an unnerving blend of the comic and the tragic that teeters into something like nihilism, an embrace of death as play, as better than life in every respect. In the latter part of *Our Mutual Friend,* she's on a rooftop, the better to see things: "You see the clouds rushing on above the narrow streets, not minding them, and you see the golden arrows pointing at the mountains in the sky from which the wind comes, and you feel as if you were dead." She's saying this to the society loan shark Fascination Fledgeby, whose roof this is and whose lackey, the Jew Riah, lives downstairs. Fledgeby, though fascinated, is discomfited:

> "How do you feel when you're dead?" asked Fledgeby, much perplexed.
> "Oh, so tranquil!" cried the little creature, smiling. "Oh, so peaceful and so thankful! And you hear the people who are alive, crying and working, and calling to one another down in the close dark streets, and you seem to pity them so! And such a chain has fallen from you, and such a strange good sorrowful happiness comes over you!"

"But you are not dead, you know," Jenny Wren adds, as though scolding him. "Get down to life!"

> Mr Fledgeby seemed to think it rather a good suggestion, and with a nod turned round. As Riah followed to attend him down the stairs, the little creature called out to the Jew in a silvery tone, "Don't be long gone. Come back, and be dead!" And still as they went down they heard the little sweet voice, more and more faintly, half calling and half singing, "Come back and be dead, Come back and be dead!"

Jenny's reverie takes place at the apex of a building consecrated to money in its ugliest aspect in the center of London's financial and mercantile district. But it's a revelation of ecstasy, not despair. It's incomprehensibly weird, which is perhaps why the BBC omitted the scene in its two adaptations of the book and why critics seem to shy away from it. It's easier to cast Jenny as eccentric, comic, and plucky in the face of challenging circumstances, another Dickensian oddball, world-weary, exemplifying fortitude in the face of suffering.

But I think Jenny is a prophet, a harbinger of what is to come when the controlling dynamics of *Our Mutual Friend*'s world reach their inevitable culmination in the triumph of consumption and waste. Like Dickens, she's a Marxist, save that her society's contradictions will birth not a worker's paradise but a heaven in which death has triumphed over life: no more shit, no more pain, all the suffering engendered by money gone, swept before the bliss of nonexistence in a joyous catastrophe.

In *Our Mutual Friend*, as money sets about destroying people— being "ruined" is inevitable whether you lose or gain a fortune— it breeds not just greed but assorted pathologies that are best called perversions. They combine obsession with self-abnegation: with social climbing, of course, and its concomitant toadying and shame that shades into prostitution. Bella almost cheerfully confesses this to her birth father over lunch beside the river (it is always the river) as she looks out and passes into a reverie parallel to Jenny's:

> And then, as they sat looking at the ships and steamboats making their way to the sea with the tide that was running down, the lovely woman imagined all sorts of voyages for herself and Pa. Now, Pa, in the character of owner of a lumbering square-sailed collier, was tacking away to Newcastle, to fetch black diamonds to make his fortune with; now, Pa was going to China in that handsome three-masted ship, to bring home opium . . . and to bring home silks and shawls without end for the decoration of his charming daughter. . . . Now a merchant of immense wealth (name unknown) had courted and

married the lovely woman, and he was so enormously rich that everything you saw upon the river sailing or steaming belonged to him, and he kept a perfect fleet of yachts for pleasure, and that little impudent yacht which you saw over there, with the great white sail, was called The Bella, in honour of his wife, and she held her state aboard when it pleased her, like a modern Cleopatra.

Then Bella tells her father her purpose in life, making what might have been shameful shameless:

> "I have made up my mind that I must have money, Pa. I feel that I can't beg it, borrow it, or steal it; and so I have resolved that I must marry it."
>
> [Her father] cast up his eyes towards her, as well as he could under the operating circumstances, and said in a tone of remonstrance, "My dear Bella!" . . .
>
> "Yes, Pa, that is the state of the case. If ever there was a mercenary plotter whose thoughts and designs were always in her mean occupation, I am the amiable creature. But I don't care. I hate and detest being poor, and I won't be poor if I can marry money."
>
> "But, my dear Bella, this is quite alarming at your age."
>
> "I told you so, Pa, but you wouldn't believe it," returned Bella, with a pleasant childish gravity. "Isn't it shocking?"

The pathology of Bella's benefactor is perhaps even more perverse. The Golden Dustman becomes a miser, a student and connoisseur of miserliness, tracking down histories and biographies of misers, titles like *Merryweather's Lives and Anecdotes of Misers*, featuring "The Miser's Mansion. The finding of a treasure. The Story of the Mutton Pies. A Miser's Idea of Death. Bob, the Miser's cur. Griffiths and his Master. How to turn a penny. A substitute for a Fire. The Advantages of keeping a Snuff-box. The Miser dies without a Shirt," and, not least, "The Treasures of a Dunghill":

One of Mr Dancer's richest escritoires was found to be a dungheap in the cowhouse; a sum but little short of two thousand five hundred pounds was contained in this rich piece of manure; and in an old jacket, carefully tied, and strongly nailed down to the manger, in bank notes and gold were found five hundred pounds more.

The Golden Dustman practically drools at this passage, and it's hard to guess which is most intense: his obsession with hoarding, with meanness, or with coprophilia.

These passages are to me, together with Jenny Wren's reverie, the most vivid, seriocomic, and horrifying in *Our Mutual Friend*. It's not quite convincing when Dickens, in the final third of the book, reforms Bella in a chapter or two and reveals the Golden Dustman's miserliness to have been a ruse to bring Bella and the hero/heir together in marriage. But Dickens has done too good a job earlier in portraying these characters against the book's dark, nihilist mood and setting for me to buy these sudden reversals.

Even Jenny Wren undergoes a sort of cure a few chapters from the end of the book, a lessening of her ecstatic death-obsessed spectral visions. Asked if she still sees "my long bright slanting rows of children, who used to bring me ease and rest . . . who used to take me up, and make me light," she responds, "I never see them now, but I am hardly ever in pain now." But I don't believe it. On her rooftop, in the immensity of her suffering, she has gone too far; she can't come back.

Reviewing *Our Mutual Friend*, the young Henry James didn't believe it either:

What do we get in return for accepting Miss Jenny Wren as a possible person? . . . Miss Jenny Wren is a poor little dwarf, afflicted, as she constantly reiterates, with a "bad back" and "queer legs," who makes dolls' dresses, and is for ever pricking at those with whom she converses, in the air, with her needle, and assuring them that she knows their "tricks and their manners." Like all Mr Dickens's pathetic characters, she is a little monster; she is deformed, unhealthy, unnatural; she belongs to the troop of hunchbacks, imbeciles, and precocious children who have carried on the sentimental business in all Mr Dickens's novels.

Of course, James is after bigger game than the plausibility of Dickens's character. He was ten years away from writing his own first novel, but he was serving notice that "attention must be paid" to his own rising generation:

> It were, in our opinion, an offence against humanity to place Mr Dickens among the greatest novelists. For, to repeat what we have already intimated, he has created nothing but figure. He has added nothing to our understanding of human character. He is master of but two alternatives: he reconciles us to what is commonplace, and he reconciles us to what is odd.

The nucleus of James's complaint is that *Our Mutual Friend* is "a book so intensely *written*, so little seen, known, or felt." It's an odd objection, knowing as we do the dense, even impenetrable verbosity and formalism that James's later work will be accused of. I'm closer to agreeing with him in saying that the book has genuine failings in its credibility, but—excluding the clumsiness of Dickens's backpedaling at the end—it's also true that the world of this book isn't quite real, is not a place that we can easily go. It's a bleak vision, frequently played for comedy or the absurd, which perhaps only increases the unease that the novel induces in me: its insistence that disaster is just around the corner and cannot be evaded, not even, despite Dickens's efforts, by sleight of hand.

James's agenda was surely in part oedipal; he meant to overthrow the authority of his parents' generation of writers. James's own father was a dotty, not to say Dickensian, figure for whom James had not much use; fathers don't play much role in his novels, save as sources of the remittances that permit his characters to live in Europe without working. His men are autonomous and deracinated, as though they don't quite come from anywhere or anyone; when they are good, they mean well without quite the vigor necessary to do well. His women are more resourceful and self-determining but seem as motherless as his men are father-less. There are mothers in his writing, but they're scarcely moth-erly; they don't nurture, console, or advise; they scheme, gossip, and broker marriages.

James was one of the first authentically modern novelists, but these models of parenting and parentage are essentially Victo-rian—in fact, typically Dickensian. Where mothers are good they are also a little weak; they need their sons to tend and admire them; really, to father them. Here's how David Copperfield, Dick-ens's most autobiographical character, describes his:

> my mother gathers some [fruit] in a basket, while I stand by, bolting furtive gooseberries, and trying to look unmoved. A great wind rises, and the summer is gone in a moment. We are playing in the winter twilight, dancing about the parlour. When my mother is out of breath and rests herself in an elbow-chair, I watch her winding her bright curls round her fingers, and straitening her waist, and nobody knows better than I do that she likes to look so well, and is proud of being so pretty.

Her son adores her, dances with her, knows she's at once inno-cent and vain, that she's a sweet coquette. She's like *Our Mutual Friend*'s Bella at her best, which she does not become until the end of the novel, when she comes into money.

Likewise, Dickens's father figures, when not tyrannical and sadistic, are similarly kind but ineffectual, not quite able to get beyond themselves and penetrate the reality of other people. They're also dotty and obsessed like *David Copperfield*'s Mr. Dick, who has spent decades laboring over an unfinishable book called *The Memorial* and whose only consolation is flying his kite:

The patience and hope with which he bore these perpetual disappointments . . . but not when he was out, looking up at the kite in the sky, and feeling it pull and tug at his hand. He never looked so serene as he did then. I used to fancy, as I sat by him of an evening, on a green slope, and saw him watch the kite high in the quiet air, that it lifted his mind out of its confusion, and bore it (such was my boyish thought) into the skies. As he wound the string in, and it came lower and lower down out of the beautiful light, until it fluttered to the ground, and lay there like a dead thing, he seemed to wake gradually out of a dream; and I remember to have seen him take it up, and look about him in a lost way, as if they had both come down together, so that I pitied him with all my heart.

Again, David shows a tender regard for what amounts to the older adult's frailty and fragility. Their kindness is linked not to virtue or strength but to eccentricity and helplessness. *Our Mutual Friend* has some good older men in it, but they, too, are a little impotent in the manner of Bella's father or act as guardians, like the Golden Dustman before he succumbs to miserism. They can be loved but not quite respected. The one fully developed father in the book is unseen: the deceased owner of the dust heaps whose last testament—his *will*, in the strongest sense of the word—has enslaved everyone whose life it touches. It is a patrimony—again, the word in its strongest sense—that castrates men and turns women into whores.

Jenny Wren is perhaps the sum of all this. Motherless from birth, she has raised herself, an adult from infancy forward. She's fatherless too: her father lives with her but as her "child," whom she disciplines and doles out her shillings to—in pretty well every sense, she's his father. Victorian society was deeply and conventionally patriarchal in its sexism and social conventions but subterraneanly trafficked in a sort of perversion of patriarchy, an antifatherhood.

Maybe that is why I am drawn to Jenny Wren. My own mother was narcissistic and childish yet adorable, rather like David Copperfield's. I danced with her more than once, tended her, but could not quite love her. My father had disappeared entirely, into a death from whence he dispensed me his shillings, not a fortune as in *Our Mutual Friend* but enough to tie me not to him but to his money. The money left me to my own devices, a pseudo-adult, able to do what I wanted without much sense of what it might be.

Nor did I imagine the childhood in an afterlife that Jenny did for herself; I couldn't conjure up any rows of golden, white-gowned children bidding me to come play with them. It would have taken a certain courage to do that. Jenny had no money except what she earned by making dresses for dolls, whereas I did: money from the afterlife, you might say. That is where redemption is supposed to occur, an end to loss and pain and want, and it did indeed save me from the last of these. But I think it took my courage in exchange, a certain capacity to be in the world and make choices about what to do in it with conviction and heart; to live fully. But I had one foot in my father's grave, in "the great black river."

I wasn't picturing my life in London in that way, not yet. I was caught up in the world of *Our Mutual Friend*—one imagined reality is surely as good as another—so off I went to photograph the "places" of the novel. I had given myself three weeks to do it: I set myself up in a nice apartment in Islington—again, the *money*—and bought twenty rolls of film and a carbon-steel tripod.

This was all top-flight equipment. My first camera as a boy had a broken viewfinder with which you could more or less frame the composition but could make out none of the details; the second one I dropped in a lake. I developed and printed in a former coal cellar: my finished photographs were speckled with motes of coal dust, with veils of brown discoloration from exhausted fixer, curled at the corners, pasty-faced for want of exposure and contrast. But they made me terribly happy. I might have been Mr.

Dick flying his kite or Dickens's mother, pretty and content in her ingenuous conceit.

Now, almost fifty years later, I had bought what had then been my dream camera, a Hasselblad, the camera used by my professional idols of the 1960s: the one David Hemmings used in *Blow Up* with his models and swinging London It Girls. It cost a couple of thousand then; now I'd picked one up for less than half that (and in devalued 2014 dollars), obsolete in the digital era. As I carried my new gear through London some of that boy came back to me, a boy parading with a grown man's camera, the sophisticated optics a bit lost on him, its artistic potential beyond his grasp. On my first day out at the site of the dust mounds near King's Cross Station I may have seemed an absurd, even suspicious character. When I set up my tripod on the sidewalk outside the headquarters of the *Guardian* newspaper, an official from the lobby came out and asked me what I was up to. These are the people who published and protected Edward Snowden, I thought to myself, but are nervous about me—maybe imagine I might be a security risk. The official was not curious but politely interrogatory.

I told him that I was doing some "street photography." I was not going to get into the business of dust mounds or Dickens: it would be too complicated to explain or maybe, I sensed, not quite believable, an unconvincing cover. He nodded and went back inside, turning once to look back at me.

In any case, I saw no sign that the dust mounds had been here. The whole area was massively built up with office towers and apartments, in furious motion with red buses, black cabs, and a torrent of pedestrians. I quickly gave up trying to take a shot of the empty street and stuck with my plan to make long exposures on slow film, holding the shutter open for up to a second. What I got in the final prints were static buildings overlaid with streaks and nebulous smears of vehicles and people. Let them be ghosts, I decided, ghosts of a future where there are no dust mounds anymore, where dust mounds exist only in books for Mr. Dick and his ilk, one of whom is me, searching for trash. As I took my pictures,

Site of the dust mounds. Photograph by author.

the wind and traffic whipped McDonald's wrappers into the air: they fell like ash and collected along the sidewalks and in the gutters.

Then I went to the river, for days at a time. Limehouse, Shadwell, London Bridge, Southwark Bridge, and more; the tide in and the tide out, the river slurping along its embankments or pulled back on itself, exposing piers and stones scummed green on the banks. The Victorian river would have stunk, of course, but even now, much cleaner, the water ran turbid, pocked and ruched with eddies and slopping wavelets, viscous and gray-green. And that is what I ended up photographing: rocks and rack on the foreshore, vortices whorling and sucking, stakes and wood bollards stuck into the bank where once upon a time someone moored a skiff or a tender. Even in full sun, under a blue sky, I could see what Dickens saw: the death the river flowed toward and its huge indifference to its mortal cargoes—corpses, waste, scavengers. It was not a river that you should ever turn your back on.

Sometimes, lugging my camera home, I felt the street closing in on me: around Hanover Square, where the Golden Dustman bought his mansion and began to hoard his shillings; in Clerkenwell, where I'd gone down a curving lane looking for a likely original of Mr. Venus's shop of morbid curiosities; or in Holloway, searching for a cottage that might have been Bella's family's before she came into money. There the white "villas" (really only stuccoed semidetached houses) seemed to lean in toward me and grow taller, disdainful and threatening. Much Victorian architecture is about height—not soaring height as you see it in a skyscraper or a medieval cathedral—but looming height, achieved by piling strata upon bricked strata of Gothic elevations and decorative doodads; height that bears downward as much as upward, that crushes as much as reaches for the sky, that might almost be under water. That, I think, accounts for the menace and spookiness in Victorian buildings and cityscapes, my sense that they must contain child laborers at work on steam looms overseen by censorious clergy, hanging judges, and cruel schoolmasters; harbor bankers and officials inured to suffering; house writers and artists who, despairing in attics, open the gas stopcock and lie down to die; conceal toothless prostitutes and stifled middle-class wives dosing themselves with laudanum.

But I love you, I wanted to respond to the buildings, to the rooms that I know are empty but that I could see myself inhabiting. I've come to pay homage, and I often believe I belong here, in the world you enclose. I'm making a likeness of you. I'm God-fearing and respectable. I have a modest fortune. I come in peace, with my faith in you. Open your doors.

Then there's the building that Dickens describes in *Our Mutual Friend*: "a very hideous church with four towers at the four corners, generally resembling some petrified monster, frightful and gigantic, on its back with its legs in the air." This church in Smith Square is the place where we first meet Jenny Wren, "a child—a dwarf—a girl—a something," who introduces herself as "the person of the house." Asked if there are any other children in the neighborhood, she cries out in disgust.

> "Don't talk of children. I can't bear children. I know their tricks and their manners. . . . Ever so often calling names in through a person's keyhole, and imitating a person's back and legs. Oh! I know their tricks and their manners. And I'll tell you what I'd do, to punish 'em. There's doors under the church in the Square—black doors, leading into black vaults. Well! I'd open one of those doors, and I'd cram 'em all in, and then I'd lock the door and through the keyhole I'd blow in pepper. . . . And when they were all sneezing and inflamed, I'd mock 'em through the keyhole."

The church is what I photographed—I had no way of guessing which house along the square might have been the model for Jenny's. The black doors were still there, less doors than blanks in the crypt wall, replicas of doors set into the stone. There was a burglar alarm above one, and the door itself had gray louvers in it and a sign saying that it must not be blocked. But no one was likely to come in or go out, not even Jenny's rascals, noses inflamed, slain by the power of her mockery. As much as she wanted to play with the celestial children, she wanted revenge.

The last place I went was to St. Mary Axe, the site of Jenny's rooftop reverie. It was in the City of London, together with Wall Street the financial capital of the world. In *Our Mutual Friend* it houses Fascination Fledgeby's loan-shark operation, "not the liveliest object

Entrance to crypt, St. Johns, Smith Square. Photograph by author.

even in Saint Mary Axe—which is not a very lively spot—with a sobbing gaslight in the counting-house window, and a burglarious stream of fog creeping in to strangle it."

There was no such building now. What had risen in its place was Norman Foster's futuristic "Gherkin" (as it's known in Lon-

St. Mary Axe. Photograph by author.

don), which houses investment banks, currency traders, brokers in futures, and assorted stock and bond traders. It looked like a zeppelin standing on its nose or, more aptly, a financier's upright fat cigar.

I set up my camera, thinking, "This is too perfect," which, indeed, the too-perfect can be: glib and obvious irony, insight on the cheap. But all the strands of *Our Mutual Friend* did seem to come together there: money, of course; Jenny's heavenly rooftop displaced by a skyscraper; even the manhole covers in the street under which shit might percolate down to the River of Death. The photos were pretty good, I thought afterward. One showed a blaze of white where a car streaked by and, next to the Lloyds

Bank Branch by the church, two ghostly figures, gesticulating. In another, I'd framed the Gherkin looming hard over a smaller building that did indeed seem to have a rooftop where people might have reveries, probably about making a killing in derivatives or, alternatively (should things head south), leap to their death and awake to find themselves playing, ascending skyscraper-high, among golden children.

All that while, I was still dating. It was October, and I was rereading the corresponding installment of *Our Mutual Friend* that had been published in October 1864, the chapter in which Jenny Wren is introduced and the first of her visions is recorded. I'd just met Janey the Madwoman, as I came to think of her. She was from an old and distinguished literary family from the fringes of the aristocracy with connections to Victorian Cambridge and later the Bloomsbury Group and beyond. Based on the first few messages we exchanged, she was also a gifted and funny writer, and she caught any and all of my references to Victorian culture and pretty much any book I thought to mention.

Janey lived in Suffolk. Since I was in London, she suggested that we might rendezvous in Cambridge, a congenial midpoint between us. We met at the Fitzwilliam Museum and didn't stay long, preferring, as we agreed, to go on a long and somewhat aimless walk. She'd show me where she grew up and where some of the Victorians and Bloomsbury writers I was intrigued by lived. Cambridge was where the bulk of them were educated, mostly at Trinity and Kings colleges. Several were members of the Apostles, an elite college society dedicated to fine conversation and, in the Bloomsbury era, the pursuit of what its members called "the Higher Sodomy," the notion that homosexuality was not only equal to but better than heterosexuality, at least when practiced by refined intellectuals and artists.

So we made our way to Kings, and that was where Janey first got tetchy. We wanted to enter the grounds in the direction of Henry VIII's famous chapel but were told by a guard that they were closed. Janey did not like this: she knew that these limitations had been imposed in response to burgeoning mobs of tourists attracted to Cambridge in recent years, for the essential reason that they were making study and ordinary college life for the fellows and students close to impossible. But Janey was a Cambridge native and this was the college of her family (the men in it, at least): surely she ought to be allowed in. The guard apologized but stood his ground. Janey, while not quite chastising him, lamented the state that things had come to these days, furiously and rather loudly. I was becoming slightly embarrassed and tried to steer her away, saying that I didn't really need to see the college. As we departed, she was still muttering and fuming.

We were more successful in seeing the riverside house formerly occupied by the descendants of Charles Darwin, who were also at the heart of the Bloomsbury set. We couldn't go in—it was still a private residence—but we sat on the bank and watched the boats go up and down the stream, undergraduates "punting," propelling their skiffs with a long pole, just as they might have done one hundred years before. I was content, and Janey was no longer seething.

Afterward we went to a cafe on the high street for a late lunch, where we got into trouble again. Nothing on the menu quite suited Janey. This put her out, and she communicated it to the waiter; not belligerently, not as though it were his fault, but, again, as a general denunciation of things being other than they should be. She did find a sandwich on the menu that, with highly specific alterations, could work for her. I ordered a salad. We talked, probably about dating—something about online dating promotes sharing accounts of the worst or oddest person you've encountered there—and then about our marriages and how we viewed our prospects, what each of us was "looking for."

I tried to articulate what that might be in my own case. When I stopped, she said, "You don't seem to *want* anything." I sensed that this wasn't a winning trait in her view and attempted to say what it was I *did* want. I came up with contentment and, of course, a relationship, wondering if that would do.

Our lunch was a long time coming. Fearing that this might promote more pique from Janey, I went not just to investigate the source of the delay but to ensure that Janey's order was being made to her specifications. It was and eventually arrived. Afterward we walked to the station, discussing whether the cafe was any good or was a disgrace. Janey took the latter view, while I poured oil on the waters and made excuses: every restaurant has bad days; maybe they were short of staff; maybe they were overwhelmed by a surfeit of customers on what was a beautiful autumn Sunday. Janey wasn't buying any of this. It was an awful place, insidious in charging what it did for a menu that was a thoughtless and sloppy fraud. Moreover, it was—of course—symptomatic of the present-day awfulness of Cambridge, of Britain, of the world.

Still, we kissed at the station. I got on my train feeling hopeful, thinking we had a connection, a frisson, or at least an affinity or two. Over the next two and a half weeks we exchanged several dozen e-mails. She recommended a book by the early twentieth-century novelist Rose Macaulay. I read it straight away and sent her my favorite passages. Janey and I, if not devout, were both attached to the Anglo-Catholic religion or at least to the writers who had attached themselves to it—reactionaries pushing back against the scientism and secularism that arose with so much drama during and in the wake of the Victorian era; ritualist esthetes, simultaneously modernists and romantics. It wasn't that they truly mourned the loss of Christian doctrine but that it made them, well, tetchy, grumpy in the mode of Jenny Wren, perhaps in the mode of Janey.

It was then that I began to slip up and with Jenny Wren that I finished the job. First, I sent Janey a web link that I thought was germane to Macaulay or some such and got back a stiff if cordial notice that Janey did not like receiving links or, especially, attachments. She didn't even open them; they muddled her, cluttered up her mailbox, made her feel the weight of obligations that she'd never asked for. When I suggested that I come up to Suffolk to visit her and her town, rather as we'd done in Cambridge, she made it clear that she didn't want that— it would be a sort of invasion: too much, too soon, if ever. She said that she'd be coming to London soon, but over the next few weeks she was beset by a series of vague ailments and distractions. By this time, I was well into the October 1864 installment of *Our Mutual Friend* and was discovering Jenny Wren and her own aches and pains. I wrote Janey and asked—amusingly, I thought—if she, too, suffered from "queer" legs and had a Bad Child who was perpetually coming home shitfaced and requiring attention. Then I sent her one of the illustrations from the original edition, showing Jenny wagging her finger, remonstrating with the Bad Child. Yes, I knew it was an attachment, but such a delightful one: what could be the harm?

Janey wrote back, friendly enough: no, her legs weren't queer and there was no Bad Child in her life. Then the e-mail switched gears: Had I tried to call her? The phone had been ringing while she was trying to rest. She was pretty sure it must be me and asked that I not do this without clearing it with her in advance. I hadn't called, though; I didn't even have her number. A further paragraph said that she didn't "feel the things that would lead to a closer connection" and that she needed to sever communications, at least for the moment. I never heard from her again. I comforted myself with the knowledge that she was obviously deeply neurotic, even a tad paranoid; a madwoman in Victorian parlance. But what she had said about my not *wanting* anything still rankled, troubling me as I tried to parse it, to tease out what it was I *should* want. Her finger went on wagging at me as I sat befuddled, hapless, muddled before her. It was I, I guessed, who was the Bad Child: a father who wanted to be a son, a boy.

Dickens nearly died while writing *Our Mutual Friend*. He was traveling home from France with his mistress, Ellen Ternan, carrying the manuscript of the novel's sixteenth installment, when his train from Folkstone derailed near Staplehurst, Kent. They survived, but ten other passengers were killed. Dickens was among those who tended the forty injured, reviving them with brandy from his flask. Afterward he returned to the overturned rail carriage and retrieved Ellen and the manuscript, although two pages were lost.

The installment that he recovered from the wreck also marks the place where *Our Mutual Friend* fully shifts from the dark vision of its first two-thirds toward a conventionally "Dickensian" conclusion. The Golden Dustman sends off the most avaricious and duplicitous of his high-society friends, and Bella at last marries the hero, still ignorant of the riches that he is inheriting. Perhaps that dramatic turn was a kind of failure of nerve or at least a manifestation of Dickens's own mixed feeling about money and also, with Ellen in hand, love. Just then he'd been showering her with jewelry, had bought her a house, and had set her up with a trust fund. The dangers of money were a problem for other people; they wouldn't spoil him or those close to him. That seems to be reflected in *Our Mutual Friend*'s confused, not to say incoherent, denouement: Bella, corrupted when enjoying the dust mound fortune in the Golden Dustman's home, is redeemed as she enjoys it when married to its rightful heir. It seems more logical that the two of them should live happily and modestly, either having never recovered the money or having renounced it in favor of, say, a charity for destitute river-men and their families. But Dickens's moral seems to be that the fortune just needed to be restored to its true legatee to undo its curse. It only needed to be in the right hands—Dickens's, perhaps.

Staplehurst was not among the worst rail disasters of the Victorian age, but it stunned the public in the way that air crashes do in our time. In Dickens's case it kept him awake at night and manifested itself in an array of psychosomatic symptoms, not least the loss of his voice immediately after the disaster. Nor could he compose: "I write two or three notes, and turn faint and sick." The sound of wheels on pavement made him anxious. The only way he could bear riding on a train—necessary for his lucrative reading tours—was to dose himself with brandy. He would die on the precise anniversary of the Staplehurst disaster five years later.

For my last batch of photos, I went back to Limehouse and the river where Dickens had first seen the poster about the drowned man. Beyond inspiring the novel, it inculcated a Mr. Venus–like fascination with corpses pulled from the river. In an essay, he described the body of a drowned woman: "The feet were lightly crossed at the ankles, and the dark hair, all pushed back from the face, as though it had been the last action of her desperate hands, streamed over the ground." He might almost have been in love, admiring those dainty ankles; might have imagined his mother, who was so light on her feet.

In Limehouse I shot color film, one of few times I'd done so over the whole trip. What stood out in the photos was less any single object or riverscape than fields and zones of green and gray, sickly green water and the gray undersides of clouds. Some of my ancestors had lived here and a bit downriver in Stepney, working as seamen and sailors, and doubtless some of them had drowned. Walking back to the tube station, I passed through the burial ground of the local church, where some of them would have been interred, assuming that their bodies had been recovered. I had to step over lighting cables and skirt crowds of extras. A Victorian drama of some kind was being filmed. In a prop truck I saw a stack of uncannily realistic severed rubber arms, legs, and heads, their presence unexplained; they might have washed up on the riverbank, come to rest along the tracks of a derailment, or fallen from the sky.

Of course, the manuscript of *Our Mutual Friend* would end up in the library of a billionaire, not just any tycoon but J. Pierpont Morgan, who made his fortune not with things—oil, steel, railroads— but with pure money, liquid money that flowed through underwriting, loans, and debentures, through currencies, flotations, and cash flows.

I went to look at the manuscript in New York and photographed it too. It contained nearly 500 pages. That's 300 fewer than in the printed edition, owing to Dickens's tiny and extraordinarily illegible handwriting. Reading the manuscript of *Our Mutual Friend* is made still more difficult by Dickens's revisions, corrections, and blottings. Fumbling through it—I was made to wear white cotton gloves—I located the rooftop scene at Saint Mary Axe but couldn't make out many of the words. Judging by the excisions and insertions, Dickens had struggled with his words. Scholars say that this was unusual, that Dickens was normally a fluent composer of nearly perfect first drafts. But in this scene he stuttered and stopped, went back and forth. Henry James might have taken this as proof that he didn't quite know what he was doing; wasn't sure what he wanted to say or who his characters were or might be becoming.

Despite that, I think Dickens got it right, at least for me. But I also don't think I really care about much in the novel now other than Jenny Wren. I'd rather not think about the money: maybe I find an antidote to it in her reverie, in sudden, effortless death and ascent. That frightens me a little: why wouldn't I—or anyone—prefer life with Bella, enjoying our fortune fully but soberly, knowing it was unearned yet unashamed of it; knowing it was just a stroke of luck, not a judgment?

Scholars who have examined the entire manuscript also note that the pages scattered and recovered from the Staplehurst crash are unstained and uncrumpled despite Dickens's assertion in the novel's afterword that they were heavily soiled. In the intervening 150 years, the dirt has apparently faded along with the paper itself, which was originally blue but now is an unremarkable shade of white.

I don't know why that should have happened. In any case, it was another disappointment. I'd wanted to encounter the manuscript and the book in its concrete form, as Dickens had made and seen it, as it had been, not as it now was. That was perhaps when I began to lose interest in *Our Mutual Friend*; when that obsession began to go the way of my preoccupation with Ruskin, Effie, and Millais. It hadn't been exhausted or completed, but, like the manuscript, simply faded away until I no longer thought about it. For a long while I didn't even notice that it was gone.

I didn't attend my father's funeral. It wasn't my choice one way or the other. I was seven, and someone must have decided I was too young or might—excitable child that I was—act out with inappropriate levity, fidgeting, whining, or fussing. I wasn't, of course, aware of the provisions of his will; nor would I be for another ten years, and then only sketchily. It would be decades until I felt their true impact, understood that they were paying for most of what I spent, or at least much more than what I earned on my own. This was not a slight thing—couldn't be ignored or shrugged off as happenstance—and had a price: its quantity altered the quality of everything it touched. It paid for the trip to England, for the camera and film, for the leisure to read *Our Mutual Friend*, for the time to write and fret about it.

My father died at Massachusetts General Hospital on the Charles River in Boston, a city founded as a kind of anti-London, a godly alternative to the mother country's greed and corruption. His ancestors would go there and become rich in spite of themselves, Golden Dustmen every one. They made their money in shipping and trade, on the water. So there he was, overlooking the river and its sluggish harbor, waiting—and not very long—for it to carry him away, leaving his money on the shore, high and dry, waiting for me to come and pick it up.

Of course, there's an antidote to all of this: renunciation. Give it away, which doesn't seem so very hard to do, really. You could take a certain pleasure in deciding who the beneficiary was to be—a home for indigent sailors; a school for photographers who haven't the wherewithal to own a Hasselblad camera; maybe mentoring for fatherless boys—and then take pride in thinking about the good it's doing. That's what you would do, what any decent person would do: you would give it away or give it back, because you would know that having it undoes the justice, the fairness, the equity, upon which human kindness and goodness are built and depend. You would, but maybe I wouldn't and won't.

But you would know better; you'd give it away, evade the river of death, the mounds of shit, the corpses in the water, the self-humiliation of miserhood or the mollycoddling bloat of trust funds and legacies, the narcissism of fancying yourself golden yet knowing you are, like everyone else, worth no more than dust. You'd know all this was an accident, a terrible accident—no more than that—as with the peregrinations of fathers and sons adrift; crashes and near-misses; the goings and comings of money and persons, persons and money; the fact that something like *Our Mutual Friend* might be your last book and, inadvertently, your legacy, your last word, your will.

Chapter 3

DIFFICULTIES

EVERY AFTERNOON in London I'd leave my apartment in Finsbury via Granville Square and descend the steps of Gwynne Place
toward King's Cross and St. Pancras Stations then ascend Swinton Street to Bloomsbury and its bookstores and the old habita-
tions of my favorite writers and artists: Dickens, of course, and
the Pre-Raphaelites in Gower Street and William Morris and
Edward Burne-Jones a little to the south in Red Lion Square, but
also their Edwardian successors, Virginia Woolf, Lytton Strachey,
E. M. Forster, John Maynard Keynes, Clive and Vanessa Bell, Duncan Grant, and more. Their one-time homes were often marked
by blue plaques or sometimes by nothing at all—Virginia Woolf's
various houses were bombed out one after the other and she fled
to the countryside. I would go and look at those places but not
photograph them, perhaps because the members of the Bloomsbury Group were not only not Victorians but, as much as anyone

could claim to be, the anti-Victorians. Still, they drew me in; I'd find myself looking their way.

What you will not notice in Bloomsbury unless you pay close attention or, forearmed with research, seek them out are the places connected to George Gissing, George Gilbert Scott Jr., or Mary Augusta Arnold Ward. You might know of Gissing via his novels *New Grub Street* or *The Odd Women* and maybe even know of Scott through his father, Sir George Gilbert Scott, who designed the Albert Memorial and St. Pancras Station, but you may not know about Mary Ward, even under the name her novels were published, Mrs. Humphry Ward. I didn't until I became an obsessive-compulsive reader of Victorian novels and discovered that Ward wrote what is likely the bestselling novel of the entire era (a million copies by some estimates): *Robert Elsmere*, published in 1888. It is not in print today, but I found a copy in a used bookstore, in Bloomsbury, of course.

Mary Ward lived on Russell Square on the present-day site of the Imperial Hotel. When the money from *Robert Elsmere* began to flow, she established a settlement house a few blocks away on Tavistock Place for the betterment of the local poor. Ward herself moved to a larger house near Buckingham Palace and then to a mansion in the country. Despite the success of *Robert Elsmere*, the upkeep of the houses and the life that went with them (not to mention a dissolute, spendthrift son) kept her continuously on the edge of bankruptcy. To stave it off, she wrote twenty-five more novels, mostly on precipitous deadlines, sustained by laudanum and cocaine. Her reputation as a social reformer, antipoverty activist, and feminist (she was instrumental in establishing the first women's college, Somerville, at Oxford) was later undercut by her opposition to female suffrage. Perhaps due to that as much as the deficiencies of her writing, she would be reviled by the Bloomsbury set as the epitome of what was wrong with the Victorians: Virginia Woolf said that "she is a menace to health of the mind as influenza is to the body"; Lytton Strachey excoriated her as "that shapeless mass of meaningless flesh—all old and insignificant."

Yet you could say that Ward was herself an anti-Victorian or at least an interrogator of its conscience and contradictions. You might imagine that to sell a million copies *Robert Elsmere* must have been a potboiler along the lines of Wilkie Collins's "sensation novels," which dealt in murder, bigamy, and the uncanny. *Elsmere* did indeed cause a sensation, not on account of explicit scenes of sex and violence but because of explicit agnosticism, loss of faith, and rejection of the church and its dogmas—"difficulties," as the Victorians customarily called the problem—closer, in their minds, to an epidemic of the age. The title character is a young Anglican priest who, under the influence of skeptical mentors (thinly veiled portraits of Oxford dons whom Ward herself had known), feels compelled to deny Christ's divinity. Now viewing Jesus as a mortal, albeit an extraordinary ethical teacher and reformer, he gives up his parish and starts a settlement house in the slums of East London. His wife, whose romance with him occupies the first third of the book, is appalled and uncomprehending but remains at his side despite her own visceral and orthodox faith. Ten years later, in *Helbeck of Bannisdale*, Ward would recast much the same plot as a love story between a deeply ascetic and devout Roman Catholic country gentleman and a beautiful agnostic. The heroine attempts conversion but cannot ultimately accept the hero's faith and commits suicide; he joins the Jesuits.

This sounds like melodrama, but Ward treated her characters' conflicts with more than sentiment. She understood their dilemmas from long-standing personal experience. Her family was as intellectually distinguished as any in England: her grandfather, Thomas Arnold, was the legendary headmaster of Rugby School and her uncle was the poet, sage, and critic Matthew Arnold. She grew up among the Oxford intelligentsia and as a girl was among Lewis Carroll's stable of photographic subjects. But her father, Tom, was a trial, a near scandal to her family by virtue of his having variously converted, lapsed, and reconverted not less than four times, shuttling between Anglicanism and Catholicism in crises of faith that resembled mental collapses. But he was no more than an extreme manifestation of the general religious crises of the moment. Ward later wrote, "Darwinism was penetrating everywhere. Pusey was preaching against its effects on belief. Balliol [College] stood for an unfettered history and criticism [of scriptural authority], Christ Church for authority and creeds." Mark Pattison, the rector of Lincoln College and model for the character in *Robert Elsmere* who persuades Elsmere to lapse, had a long-standing affair with a younger woman, but his religious opinions were every bit as notorious.

In the eyes of many, *Robert Elsmere* reflected—perhaps even seemed to precipitate—a national crisis so disconcerting that three-time prime minister William Gladstone was moved to address it in an 11,000-word essay:

> Never was a book written with greater persistency and intensity of purpose. Every page of its principal narrative is adapted and addressed by Mrs. Ward to the final aim which is bone of her bone and flesh of her flesh. The aim is to expel the preternatural element from Christianity, to destroy its dogmatic structure, yet to keep intact the moral and spiritual results.

This is not only a fool's errand, Gladstone continued, but a pernicious one, because a religion based entirely on the intellect, on reason rather than hope and belief, is no religion at all. Ward had succeeded in her mission by deploying the devices of the novel: its appeal to emotion, the seductions of drama and suspense, and the pleasure taken in the triumph of the individual over authority and institutions. Its most dangerous result was the undermining of our sense of sin, our helplessness before human frailty and evil without God's mercy. As evidence that this sense was fast eroding, Gladstone cited another work of fiction:

> In the novel of *The Unclassed*, by the author of *Thyzra*, which like *Robert Elsmere* is of the didactic and speculative class, the leading man-character, when detailing his mental his-

tory, says that "sin" has never been for him a word of weighty import. . . . [T]he negative writers of our day have formed, or at least exhibited, a very feeble estimate of the enormous weight of sin, as a factor in the condition of man and of the world.

Gladstone didn't mention *The Unclassed*'s author—perhaps didn't want to dignify the novel with one—but it was George Gissing.

Walking to Bloomsbury, I often passed by one of George Gissing's London homes: on Swinton Street, for example, where I sometimes felt that the buildings on either side were leaning out over me, bearing down on me. One time, though, the sensation got out of hand. I thought I couldn't withstand it: I might need to seek medical or psychiatric attention. What had previously seemed an optical illusion was now a full-on hallucination, so vivid that I had to concentrate on maintaining my belief that it was no more than that. At the same time, I felt that the boundary between me and the exterior world had become porous and was fast disappearing: sensations—all the things we filter or exclude so as not to have our perceptual apparatus overwhelmed—poured in as my thoughts seemed to be leaching out, replaced by notions and impressions that didn't feel like my own. In the moment the best I could manage was to force myself to cling to the thought that none of it was real, that it would stop soon.

It did stop. The whole episode probably only lasted ten or twenty seconds. The flood withdrew; the daylight had become ordinary again, along with the sense of subject and object, internal and external, me in the world, but distinct from it. It had been no more than an eclipse: for a moment everything had been utterly altered but was then put back the way it was. I'd experienced a moment of terror and vertigo: temporarily losing my footing in the real world and being thrown into one where things were uprooted, rearranging themselves, refusing to be constrained in their customary spaces. But now buses went up and down the hill again and the road was its usual width and inclined at its normal slope; the buildings stood still, impassive but without menace.

Swinton Street. Photograph by author.

Afterward, I was inclined to avoid Swinton Street, except that I wanted to locate Gissing's house at number 62 and photograph it. It took me a while to realize that it was gone, replaced by a modern health clinic. That was not unusual, at least not in the case of Gissing: I had a list of fourteen London addresses occupied by him in the space of sixteen years, half of which had been demolished, bombed, or built over. That was Gissing's luck, both in literature and in pretty much every other aspect of his life. He was, in general, miserable, reduced where not erased entirely.

Gissing paid his dues as much as any writer I've heard of. He lived mostly in poverty, made two hellish marriages, and wrote prolifically and penetratingly about poverty and gender, which gained him neither financial security nor much reputation in his lifetime. He was beset by an onslaught of misfortune, betrayal, bad timing, and impulsive, ill-considered decisions. Born in Yorkshire in 1857 and abandoned by his father, he grew up poor but from an early age displayed such intellectual talent that he was given a full scholarship to a college in Manchester, with the expectation of a brilliant career in classics and literature. But he began to haunt the nearby slums, some of the worst in Europe. There he lost his virginity to and fell in love with a seventeen-year-old alcoholic prostitute named Nell Harrison. He aimed to reform her and to marry her. To support her and keep her off the street, he began stealing from students and faculty at his college. He was caught, expelled, and sent to the workhouse for three months. Nell had given him a ravaging case of syphilis, though it did nothing to moderate his ardor for her. On his release, he exiled himself and went to America for a year, working in anonymity as a schoolteacher and, increasingly, a writer of stories and journalism. But he didn't prosper there and returned to England in 1877, broke and depressed.

On arrival in London, he located Nell. They moved into 62 Swinton Street and shortly afterward to the other side of Bloomsbury at 22 Colville Place. That house, too, is now demolished. I went to photograph the place where it had stood, which consisted of a fence and a playground. I had no further vertigo, only disappointments, there and at another half-dozen razed Gissing sites.

Despite Gissing's best efforts, Nell increased her drinking, took up with other prostitutes and lowlifes, and soon—seemingly by force of habit, for diversion—was selling herself on the street again. Although Gissing wanted to be a socialist—to believe that behavior was a product of social conditions and could be changed for the better by improving them—his experience with Nell suggested otherwise: class and gender were destiny. It made him a fatalist for whom suffering seemed life's only constant. As a writer, his subjects would be poverty, the disappointments of political struggle, the frustrations of relationships between men and women, and the miseries of literary production.

Gissing freelanced as a tutor on Colville Street but also made a start on several aborted novels. In the end he would write twenty-three of them (sometimes two a year), but only *New Grub Street* and *The Odd Women* are much read today. He knew, though, that this would be his work's fate. He knew that he was talented but also knew that he was doomed. He would eventually be free of Nell, who went mad and was confined in Bedlam. He married another woman just as awful as her, but they had a son, who also became a writer.

It was now late October, and I'd fallen into a certain routine in my flat. Every afternoon I took pictures during what photographers call "the golden hour" (the light is redder, softer, deeper in some way, starting around four o'clock). Before that I'd walk in Blooms-bury and around St. Pancras and King's Cross Stations where *Our Mutual Friend*'s dust mounds used to be.

But in the mornings, I'd read Gissing, or rather Gissing's journals, some six hundred pages of them, and transcribe passages like these into my own journal:

Death, if it came now, would rob me of not one hope, for hopes I simply have not.

I never enjoy anything now—*never anything.*

Did nothing, and thought nothing.

In morning all but dark for half an hour. Wretched day. Did two pages, but must write them again.

Feeling stupid. Did three pages, having destroyed yesterday's. Have no confidence in this novel of mine, but must finish it, because I am all but penniless.

No sleep at night. No work to-day. Misery.

Day of blank misery.

Utter wretchedness.

Complete breakdown again. At the end of Vol. I, but feel it won't do. Wandered about in despair.

Dull weather. Did nothing; misery.

I didn't know what to make of Gissing: I wanted to believe that writing was supposed to fulfill or at least relieve a kind of internal pressure that, unspent and unreleased, led to depression, addiction, and disassociation. At the best of times, it held the promise of joy and fulfillment; of the excavation and revelation of emotional truths that lead other humans to delight, maybe tears, self-understanding, even to actions that bring some good into the world. This is what I believed—or had believed at some point in the past. Myself, I was keeping at it, pushing forward with what was becoming what you are reading now, and keeping pessimism pretty well at bay. I hadn't taken my vertigo as a warning, though I might have. I even thought it might be a sign of my engagement with my Victorians: that I was merging with what Gerard Manley Hopkins might have called their "inscape," that I was getting lost in it and would come out the other side understanding something about it. That was the hopeful view. The other one—Gissing's—was that writing was simply driving me crazy: when I attempted to translate reality into art, reality struck back hard and showed me just how futile was the effort.

So I sat at my wooden table in the mornings, getting up once or twice to walk down to the corner to an espresso bar. I would sit in the window there and look down the street toward Wilmington Square where Gissing had set one of his grim proletarian novels, *The Nether World*. Most mornings, a couple occupied the opposite table, one often holding the *London Review of Books*, the other its New York counterpart. Each usually carried a novel and a notebook. Now and again one or the other would look up from his *Review* and smile and make some apposite comment on its contents. Then they would go back to their reading and their coffees, to the literary life and its contentments.

I, though, would return to the flat, to my wasteland, the nether world of Gissing's journals. I read what he wrote about the death of Nell, freeing him from the struggle to support her, to keep her out of trouble or inside the asylum. He had come to loathe her as much as love her: she'd been the proximate cause of his expulsion from college and his subsequent penury in the squalid flats that I wanted to photograph and of the syphilis that ultimately killed him. But as her only kin he needed to go to her room to claim her body and possessions.

There were three engravings: a landscape, a piece by Landseer, and a Madonna of Raphael. There was a portrait of Byron, and one of Tennyson. There was a photograph of myself, taken years ago, to which, the landlady tells me, she attached special value, strangely enough. . . .

On the door hung a poor miserable dress and a worn out ulster; under the bed was a pair of boots. Linen she had none; the very covering of the bed had gone save one sheet and one blanket. I found a number of pawn tickets, showing that she had pledged these things during last summer—when it was warm, poor creature! All the money she received went in drink; she used to spend my weekly 15/ the first day or two that she had it. . . .

She lay on the bed covered with a sheet. I looked long, long at her face, but could not recognize it. It is more than three years, I think, since I saw her, and she had changed horribly. Her teeth all remained, white and perfect as formerly.

There was art in that room, even beauty. For all her wretchedness, she had her Raphael and her Tennyson and something recognizable from her youth lingered in her face. It was February of 1888, the year *Robert Elsmere* came out and Gladstone wrote in response about "the chasm between deity and the human soul, over which the scheme of Redemption has thrown a bridge, again yawns beneath our feet, in all its breadth and depth." Gissing, though, felt tenderness, though no guilt about Nell, no sense of sin:

> In nothing am I to blame; I did my utmost; again and again I had her back to me. Fate was too strong. But as I stood beside that bed, I felt that my life henceforth had a firmer purpose. Henceforth I would never cease to bear testimony against the accursed social order that brings about things of this kind. I feel that she will help me more in her death than she balked me during her life. Poor, poor thing!

Gissing made good on that pledge. He wrote socially conscious novels that increasingly explored the lot of women and their relationships with men—that most frustrating and intractable dilemma of his life, impossible to separate from his poverty and his failure to write the books that he felt he could write if he were free of the burdens women saddled him with.

Maybe his pity—which heretofore had seemed confined to himself—at Nell's death extended itself outward: the walls came down, the boundaries and incomprehensions became porous, less opaque than veiled. They could be rendered into writing. Failures of imagination could be overcome by looking harder and seeing more clearly, by a kind of penetrating compassion. On good days I too had a sense that writing might work this way, through love and faith in the notion that life was tragic but charged with something worth attending to and holding dear. But it was only a sense, really, a sense that I feared I was losing: a faith that seemed less tenable, less consoling; I had assumed that it accompanied me as a matter of course but, turning around (in Swinton Street?), saw that it was gone.

Unlike Gissing, if not quite to the extent of Gladstone, that faith was joined to another, more conventional religious faith. When it had come to me ten years earlier, I'd made much of it: written a book called *My Grandfather's House* about it, in fact. I was uncomfortable with the book now. I had become a Roman Catholic, the first Catholic in my family since the sixteenth-century and the English Reformation. In the interim my ancestors had been Puritans, Unitarians, Episcopalians, Transcendentalists, and agnostics. In the book I tried to imagine what their lives had been like and what my life had become in bringing my family's history full-circle. I still think that it was an interesting project. But, for all its appeals to undogmatic wonder and mystery, the book was also more than a little smug; maintained too many things as certainties; lacked the humility that makes religion loving rather than intolerant; took, in a word, too little on faith.

My adherence to religion had been ebbing away for several years, but not very consciously. Confronted with the church's positions on gender and sexuality as well as its stoking of America's culture wars, I'd looked the other way for a long while. But in the end my evasions couldn't withstand the facts: the support of Catholic intellectuals for the Bush administration's war; the church's disingenuous appeals to "religious freedom"; the cruel legalism of, for example, expelling children from parochial schools when their parents were discovered to be gay.

So there had been some principle involved. But it had more to do with what I'm reluctant to call self-pity, though, as with Gissing, that's the most honest word for it. After a long run of happiness and good fortune, things that had come easily became difficult, work laborious, love elusive when it was not a trial. It wasn't so much depression as deflation, the feeling that little by little what had been vivid in my life had been replaced by flat and muffled days that never quite seemed to dawn. God was far off, could not be touched or spoken of except by vague analogies, furnishing no "certitude, nor peace, nor help for pain," as Matthew Arnold, Mary Ward's uncle, had famously put it.

On the evening of November 5 my "difficulties" came to a head. I'd gone to see a woman in Brighton whom I'd been on two dates with. On the second, we made an excursion to Virginia Woolf's house in Sussex (the one at which she killed herself). Afterward

I was convinced that my date felt the same attraction to me that I felt for her. Going down to Brighton, I imagined that this would be openly acknowledged, that we'd move on to the next step. Instead, she announced that she could offer no more than friendship. We weren't a good fit: we were "from different tribes," she said. She had a voice that resembled the voices of British actresses I admired—silken, just faintly nasal, sly and knowing, classless but classy—which only made me wish all the more that I could be in her tribe, that I might belong with someone.

On the train back to London, I read a book about narcissism, which said that the narcissist's worldview collapses along with his defenses; thereafter his life will seem a desert for a long, long while. I didn't want it to be prophetic, but I guessed that it might be.

Walking home from St. Pancras Station, I heard firecrackers going off and I remembered that it was Guy Fawkes Night, which is a little like Halloween in America. Guy Fawkes was a militant Catholic who conspired to blow up the Houses of Parliament in 1605. His plot was foiled, and he was tortured and hung. Since then he's been commemorated in effigies that children make with old clothes and straw and with which they solicit money—"pennies for the Guy"—as a reward for their artistry. On November 5 bonfires are laid in the streets. The "Guys" are tossed onto them and burned in effigy while fireworks crack and boom.

Dejected and confused—how could I have been so wrong; why hadn't she felt what I felt?—I heard the explosions. It occurred to me that Guy Fawkes Night was really a festival of anti-Catholicism, commemorating putting heretics to the flame and crushing Catholicism in England. I didn't feel targeted—that aspect of its origins is pretty well forgotten—but I thought to myself what a night this would be to lose my faith once and for all; to drag my religion's clattering bones home to my copybook of Gissing's journals and bury them. For a moment all the failures—of faith, of love, of vision—seemed like one.

Gissing, you won't be surprised to hear, had not a shred of religious conviction. In 1882, six years before *Robert Elsmere* was published, he wrote an essay called "The Hope of Pessimism." Under the influence of Arthur Schopenhauer, he laid down a philosophy for a postreligious age founded on an acceptance of "the weariness of being," an acknowledgment that only "one fate awaits us all." A religion of art was the only possible response: as with Schopenhauer, he imagined it as a kind of Buddhist detachment: "In the mood of artistic contemplation the will is destroyed, self is eliminated, the world of phenomena resolves itself into pictures of absolute significance, and the heart rejoices itself before images of pure beauty." But the contemplation that Gissing is imagining—at least for himself—is not contemplation of the poetic sublime or the transcendent but a unflinchingly realist "picturing" that "signifies nothing more than artistic sincerity in the portrayal of contemporary life."

If Gissing indeed adopted the philosophy of "The Hope of Pessimism," it afforded him very little solace. Within a few years, his journal records "feeling terribly wretched. The struggle to get my story clear is driving me almost to madness"; then "no sleep at night. No work today. Misery"; then "Day of bleak misery." Or maybe this is what life for the artist looks like—should look like—under "The Hope of Pessimism." At any rate, four months after completing the essay Gissing had finished *New Grub Street.*

By then Gissing was in love again, this time with Edith Underwood, another working-class woman he met in the street. Her alcoholism and insanity proved as profound as Nell's. He stayed with her for eight years, largely because of the two sons she bore him, to whom he was devoted, particularly the younger of the two, Alfred. Edith was ultimately committed to an insane asylum, where she spent the rest of her life; the boys were placed with relatives for the remainder of their childhoods. Gissing moved to France, where he met a woman companion who gave him some contentment and stood at his deathbed when he died in 1903.

I suppose that Gissing was a failure in every respect except in his art—even the buildings that he lived in are mostly dust—maybe even unsuccessful in his art, if successful art entails a reasonably sized audience, a decent income, and a sense of satisfaction. So maybe it is appropriate that the one book of his that has achieved some posterity is *New Grub Street*, a novel about failing as a writer, a novel about artistic frustration and suffering. Myself, I couldn't seem to get enough of it.

Although I came to England and immersed myself in Victoriana in order to write, maybe I had in truth come here to escape from writing, anywhere that didn't face the empty page, the keyboard that spouted clichés and incoherencies. Of course in the end the mind refuses to buckle under to our evasions, to ignore the contradictions from which they are formed. Now I found myself in pursuit of a writer who worked at his art like a slave but got pretty much nowhere for his trouble. Maybe in Gissing I aimed to find consolation in the example of a writer more miserable than me, one whose career seemed like an exercise in self-flagellation. In all this maybe I was looking for reasons *not* to write, an object lesson that would justify quitting with no risk of shame or doubt. Gissing's productivity depended on manic bursts of composition, but his daily bread was accomplishing nothing except being miserable. He could be seen as the avatar of writer's block, of authorship as torture and self-annihilation. I might have been following his example in other areas too: on my dates, in wanting to join a tribe I didn't belong. I was, like Gissing, looking for precisely the wrong love, not the right love. For those purposes, I could scarcely do better than his example.

I went on photographing his places: 62 Swinton Street and 22 Colville Place were gone and so, I would find, were 31 Gower Place, 38 Edward Street, 55 Wornington Road, and more—gone. I couldn't stare at their facades, summon up Gissing at his benighted desk behind nasty tattered curtains, and think: you poor, miserable bastard. The missing houses insisted on my facing a blank canvas, asking me what, exactly, I would make out of nothing, from my own devices.

So I photographed Colville Place and the rest: shrubs and a fence with a bicycle leaning against it, blank facades and roads where there had been Georgian and Victorian row houses. Whole streets had been renamed, rerouted, or simply disappeared, sometimes beneath other roads or construction (I could find them by consulting old maps) but sometimes uncannily, as though entire locales had been spirited away. In lieu of them, I would photograph the neighborhoods where Gissing had set his fictions, most of which were in the vicinity of my flat around Islington, Finsbury, and Clerkenwell. Like so much of contemporary London, Gissing's slums are now multi-million-pound real estate: it was hard to reimagine the squalor and desperation that used to inhabit the spaces now occupied by fashionable restaurants, shops, and bars. I took to photographing blank brick walls, the screens behind which other lives transpired, real or imagined, where children once starved, where currency traders now ate locavore cuisine.

Gissing wouldn't have been surprised, I think. Not because of pessimism, but because of what amounted to his faith—deeply held—that there was no redemption, pre-Christian, Christian, or post-Christian, and no mercy. There was life as it stood, impassive before socialism or religion or good intentions.

After the woman in Brighton, I dated Alexa, whose father had been an art dealer who had written about and traded in the work of Holman Hunt. I hadn't known this when we'd met online, but I had mentioned my interest in Victoriana in my profile: she must have asked me about it. I don't know how we got onto Hunt, but I mentioned my problem with him and then she told me about her father's book, which was not just about Hunt but about *The Light of the World* in particular.

Alexa said this without much expression or emphasis; certainly with no indication that it was an amazing coincidence of the kind it seemed to me. We were sitting in the basement of a cafe in Notting Hill, stirring our coffees, volleying the questions about exes and pastimes that you ask when you're meeting someone previously known to you only online. I had been trying for a long time to get the problem of Hunt and *The Light of the World* out of my

Colville Place. Photograph by author.

mind—and then there it was, intimately connected to the woman across the table.

I wondered if I should tell her how awful I thought the painting was and how very disconcerting its awfulness—following me around, insistent—was to me. Maybe she loved the painting, if only because her father, some years deceased, had lavished so much attention on it. I wouldn't want to give offense, especially if I wanted to see her again, which I thought I might very well want to do. So instead I said that I would read his book, that I'd find a copy that very day, which I did.

I learned that there were three versions of the painting, the one I saw in Oxford being the first. The third version toured the empire just after the death of Queen Victoria and was seen by seven million people, as many as ten thousand a day. People knelt before it and wept; atheists and agnostics said that it had restored their faith. Maybe it was the ultimate Victorian masterpiece, the antidote to "difficulties," the feeling that God had withdrawn himself and that things had come undone.

But I remained unmoved. It was still awful, but I saw how very far I was from understanding the Victorians. Alexa's father hadn't tried to make a case for the painting's artistic value but for its value as a cultural phenomenon. I had to admit that he succeeded: *The Light of the World* was a force equal to *Robert Elsmere*.

I e-mailed Alexa to say how impressed I was by the book and suggested that we get together again. She wrote back that she had been dating someone else before we'd met and that in the interval that relationship had been developing; she thought she'd best concentrate on seeing where it went. That was that. I was hurt and dejected, though not with much reason: we had only, after all, met once. Maybe I'd hoped that she would finally explain the painting to me, open me up to it, teach me to love it. But instead I'd failed again, left to puzzle things out alone.

During that time, St. Pancras Station was always in view. You could see its spires and towers from the doorstep of my flat and pretty much from anywhere in Finsbury and Bloomsbury. I thought it was magnificent—the greatest Victorian building of all—but was a bit sheepish about it, as with my affection for much Victoriana. I never quite knew if it was truly magnificent or simply much too much. John Summerson, one of the essential architecture critics of the twentieth century, split the difference and called it "Sir George Gilbert Scott's tawdry masterpiece." He also admitted to finding the building "nauseating," and I think I know what he meant. Looking at it made you a bit queasy: on the one hand, its height, its ascending piles of ornament, and its ceremonial, even liturgical style made it worthy of awe; on the other, you felt suckered by its scale and pretensions into admiring what is ultimately in bad taste, not magnificent but vulgar. It is, after all, not a cathedral or a seat of government but a train station with a luxe hotel stuck on front. Scott had been commissioned to build the new Foreign Office in Whitehall, but the government refused to countenance his Gothic Revival design. It is said that he recast his ideas for that project in St. Pancras with some bitterness, perhaps indeed with the sense that the station was indeed a lesser, tawdrier piece of work.

That could not be said of the dozens of churches and cathedrals that Scott built or of the Albert Memorial, the most Victorian piece of Victoriana of all. It confounded me almost as much as *The Light of the World*: was it monumental or overbearing, stunning or elephantine (and there are elephants, in tribute to Britain's colonial possession of India), an expression of national grief or of bloated sentiment? It could have been any and all of those for me. What it was for the Victorians themselves I can't say except that they were following the lead of their queen, who was the nation's mourner-in-chief, who dressed in black for pretty much the rest of her life after the death of Prince Albert. And perhaps that suited the age and the preoccupations of her subjects: their mixed feelings about faith, progress, family and gender relations, and paternal authority were summed up in this manifestation of confusion; the jumble of ornament and motifs, an art fully convinced only of its desire to ascend and make a weighty impression on the earth, but ascend toward what? I went to photograph it once but only shot close-ups of the elephants: the thing *in toto* was too much. It would have been preposterous were it not also somehow diffident, a monument not just to loss but, it seemed to me, a sort of failure, an imperial gesture touched by perplexity.

Scott finished up the most prominent and doubtless richest architect of the Victorian age and launched a dynasty via his son, George Junior, and grandson, Giles Gilbert, who designed Liverpool Cathedral, the Thames powerhouse that now houses the Tate Modern, and, not least, the ubiquitous red telephone kiosks found throughout the nation. But it was George Junior who interested me most, the one whom architectural historians said was the most gifted of the three, who most deeply plumbed the possibilities of the Gothic Revival and foreshadowed those of modernism. Unlike his father, he did not produce many finished buildings; and, as with Gissing, only a handful of those still stand. He was an intellectual magpie and a wayward Catholic convert. He

St. Pancras Hotel and Station. Photograph by author.

died alcoholic, broke, and insane, estranged from his children just as he had been from his own father, in a bedroom in the St. Pancras Hotel. He was, perhaps you will say, my cup of tea. I'd read everything (which was not very much) about him and went to photograph his places.

Scott Junior is supposed to have built seven or eight churches and chapels, a larger number of houses and rectories, and some college buildings. He went to work in his father's practice after attending Eton, supervising some of the firm's projects and church restorations. After working on one of these at Cambridge, he was inspired to enroll as a student, earning a "first" and then a fellowship at Jesus College after winning a prize for an essay on "The Intellectual Character of the First Cause, as Affected by Recent Investigations of Physical Science," which aimed to defend the idea of divine origin of creation against Darwinism.

Unlike many Victorian sons—especially sons of successful fathers—Scott was not a rebel or antiauthoritarian, at least not in a conventional sense. His politics were Tory and became more conservative over time; and, as the essay showed, his Christian belief remained intact. It was, in fact, his deepening and intensifying faith—ending in Roman Catholicism—that would make him a black sheep. It also informed his architecture, which rejected the High Victorian style of his father and his generation for a more austere late medieval English Perpendicular Gothic that he felt was better suited to worship as conducted by Anglo-Catholics and Roman Catholics. But it was precisely the churches that embodied his approach most successfully that were gone, damaged by bombing in World War II, considered beyond repair, and pulled down. That would not stop me from photographing them, or at least the places where they had stood. I was beginning to like photographing such absences, or at least not feeling frustrated or overly disappointed by them. It seemed to allow me to make a special claim upon them; to be seeing what other people couldn't see, to be peering into a world that belonged solely to me.

I went on a date with another woman, also an art historian, a specialist in Victorian photography. After we'd had coffee at the Tate Britain, communing with some daguerreotypes and a couple of whopping Turners, we agreed to meet up at a Scott church in Camberwell in south London. I think she was just as keen as me: it was she who had known about the church and had always wanted to see it.

We were meant to meet on a Sunday, but it was raining hard. I told her not to bother coming; that we would do it another time. But I went by myself, though I cannot say why. I checked the timetables and saw that the closest train station was Denmark Hill, close by the site of the house that Ruskin grew up in. It was a place I should photograph.

I knew that the house was gone: it had been razed and the grounds turned into a public park. But I was not prepared for how absolutely it had been erased: the site was now on a faceless road of turn-of-the-century suburban "villas" with only a car wash and a filling station standing out against the rain and the gray. I found a tiny marker indicating that this was the location of the Ruskin house and stood next to it: sopping, my camera sheltered under my coat, staring down a driveway bordered by shrubs, with a big Mercedes parked at the end.

I never got to the church, which, it turned out, was not by George Gilbert Scott Jr. at all but by his father. My date's source had been wrong. As ever, where Scott Junior's work was not obliterated it was misattributed and, in any case, overshadowed by his father's: eight hundred buildings against the son's dozen or so. His father's works constituted an entire outline of Victorian society, making up the stages and scenery of my novels and obsessions and vertigoes: his 143 churches (either designed or rebuilt), of course, to hold all that faith and unfaith; 40 workhouses for the likes of Dickens's father and everyone one else who failed to have money; Reading Gaol for sexual and gender misfits like Oscar Wilde; even 4 lunatic asylums for Gissing's wives and, as it would turn out, for Scott Junior himself.

Of course, the site of the Ruskin house had not really been Ruskin's place but his father's. There are always fathers, even (maybe especially) in their deepest absences. But, to me, nowhere so strikingly as in the Victorian age with its beards and seers and Old Testament thunderers and "driving" amassers of wealth, overseen by the Queen, a small but formidable woman who adored her husband, Albert, like a daddy's girl, and had him memorialized on an uncanny, perhaps absurd, scale by Scott Junior's father.

A few days later, I went to Ramsgate on the English Channel. There, too, Scott Junior had been slighted: another building of his own was mistakenly attributed to his father. It was a chapel in the municipal cemetery on the fringe of an ugly neighborhood.

One grimy late Victorian row house, bristling with old television antennas and fronted by a mismatched door, had a sign on it reading "Polite Notice." But I couldn't discern what the notice might refer to or what it meant to say: "Go Away"? "Don't Loiter Here"? "Don't Look"?

The cemetery had a long drive that led straight down to the chapel, which was shaped like a squared cross with a tower at the center. The tower, though, was taller on one side than the other, topped on the left by a smaller secondary tower. To the right of this was a window, off-center. It seemed to me that this arrangement should throw off the balance of the whole structure. The windows on the nave below the tower were also out of kilter and of different shapes and proportions. It ought to have seemed lopsided and clumsy and hodgepodge, but it didn't. It was a rebellious building, flouting the rules of Victorian Gothic—Scott's father's architecture—and getting away with it for reasons I couldn't put my finger on. I tried to go in, but the door was locked. I photographed a piece of exterior wall, a downspout, and the trees behind the building. Their limbs ran all in one direction, away from the sea, contorted by a perennial wind that was not blowing when I was there.

The other reason I had come to Ramsgate was to visit the Grange, the home of another architect, Augustus Pugin. It was less a house than a compound, around which Pugin had grouped a church, cottages, and a full-fledged monastery, a village within the larger town. Pugin was the preeminent founder of the Victorian Gothic Revival and George Gilbert Scott's chief inspiration: "the thunder of Pugin's dreams" had been his creative epiphany, Scott said. For Pugin, Gothic was more than a style; it was a complete manifestation of England, of English culture, of medieval communitarianism built around social cohesion, obligation, labor and craft, and charity, with the church at its core. He was a brilliant architect and designer—he'd been the co-builder of the Houses of Parliament—but, still more, he was an aesthete and a passionate Catholic convert, a man in constant pursuit of beauty and the divine. As an acquaintance wrote, "he rushed into the

George Gilbert Scott Jr., Ramsgate Cemetery Chapel. Photograph by author.

arms of a church which, pompous by its ceremonies, was attractive to his imaginative mind."

I went overboard at the Grange, rushing into its arms. I photographed inside and out, in black-and-white and color: hallways, roofscapes, fireplaces, a bed and its coverlet in the master suite, a flagon and an empty holy water stoop by the door of Pugin's private chapel. I shot until I ran out of film, until I was sated. As with other Victorian buildings that had drawn me in, even obsessed me, after a while I felt overwhelmed, swamped in detail, in crockets and pointed arches and saturated polychrome and gilded decorations. I was submerged, and the water was pouring in. It was like Swinton Street: an attic-full of accreted gorgeousness, a jum-

Augustus Pugin, the Grange. Photograph by author.

ble of marvelous doodads and bric-a-brac, was closing over my head. Walking back to the station, I knew that I now had seen a place that I'd sought for a long time: it had been beautiful, yet for some reason I had no desire ever to return.

Pugin's counterpart inside the church was undoubtedly John Henry Newman, the Anglican priest whose conversion to Roman Catholicism and elevation to a cardinalship stunned the Victorian world. Medievalism and the Gothic were the artistic and cultural expression of the "Oxford Movement" (in which Newman had been the leading figure) to return the English church to its pre-Reformation roots. In fact, much of the opposition to the

Gothic Revival in architecture was based less on artistic considerations than on the fear that it was a sort of aesthetic stalking horse for Roman Catholicism.

Victorian faith was under threat from two opposing sides: Darwin and the agnosticism explored by Mrs. Humphry Ward on one and defections to the Roman church by prominent figures like Newman on the other. Rationalism and neo-medieval piety jointly pressed upon a national Anglican Church increasingly incapable of inspiring rudimentary allegiance, never mind devotion. For every expression of religious doubt or renunciation by people like George Eliot, Ward, Ruskin, and Gissing there seemed to be a concomitant conversion to Catholicism by a prominent academic, writer, or clergyman. Newman himself had received the likes of Gerard Manley Hopkins, among others.

Another convert was George Gilbert Scott Junior. His father had been a devout architectural follower of Pugin but had never felt the need to follow him into the Roman church or even Anglo-Catholicism. It was Scott Junior—a rebel against Pugin's strictures on the primacy of late medieval style—who "went over." Reading his biography, however, I began to feel that his conversion was less spiritual than temperamental; that Scott Junior's general pessimism (not unlike Gissing's) arose from and in turn fed a sense of failure, lassitude, and creative stasis, a sort of disassociation: "old work was *real* . . . ours is not real, but only *like* real," said one of his contemporaries, Norman Shaw. But, as with Scott Junior's political conservatism, Catholicism did seem real, insisting on its own 1,800-year-old tradition as both authoritative and unalterable. Without it, he felt, his creative work could only be empty: "a blank skepticism, or an arbitrary agnosticism, have never, and never can, originate any advance either in art or in any other department of practical life."

Scott Junior was introduced to Newman in 1880 and shortly thereafter attended a morning mass celebrated by Newman on his behalf. Afterward he:

had not walked fifty yards down the street before as it were a momentary flash of thought passed through my mind and I saw in an instant that all the difficulties, uncertainties and indecision of years was but a phantom, and that my duty was clear as day. . . . Simply all my old difficulties fast tumbled down, in a moment, like—so to speak—a house of cards, and I had quickly made up mind to become a Catholic before I reached the second street corner.

His family was appalled, relieved only that he had waited until after his father's death two years earlier. Beyond the social embarrassment that came with his conversion, it would have an impact on the family architectural firm (now managed by his brother), which was dependent in large part on commissions from the Anglican Church.

To Scott himself, his conversion seemed utterly rational, even practical, but in the eyes of others it was a manifestation of mental instability. Those closest to him had reason to think this. His drinking—"alcoholic drink is . . . the properly & divinely designed beverage of man," he'd said—was resulting in unexplained absences, night-wanderings that sometimes ended in the company of prostitutes or in arrest. He had his first bout of mania in 1881. Within a year he was committed to the Royal Bethlem Hospital—Bedlam—afflicted with paranoid delusions. After his release, he was arrested several more times while carrying a knife for protection against his imaginary persecutors, threatening passersby with it. His family applied to have him permanently committed, but he fled to France before the judge could issue a ruling.

Scott Junior had long stretches of lucidity during his exile: "I am in a rather droll position . . . hav[ing] been declared legally a lunatic, incapable of managing my affairs in England, while here in France I have been examined by the official medicals, and have been pronounced with equal certainty to be perfectly sane." But after returning home (where his wife and two infant sons had been secreted from him in the countryside) he faced more arrests and hospitalizations. In January 1888 he was committed to St. Andrew's Hospital for Mental Diseases at Northhampton for the Middle and Upper Classes. There his room overlooked the hospital's chapel, designed by his father.

Scott Junior made several attempts to escape and was eventually released, only to relapse into his customary bouts of drinking, mania, paranoia, and run-ins with the law. He worked sporadically, mostly on his final project, the Catholic cathedral in Norwich, which his brother finished when Scott Junior became too incompetent to go on. In sum, he had produced thirteen buildings in his career against his father's eight hundred.

After 1894 there are few records and little evidence of his whereabouts. But by 1897 he was inhabiting his final quarters, a room in the St. Pancras Hotel, his father's masterpiece. He died there, according to the death certificate, of "acute cirrhosis of the liver and heart disease" and "exhaustion syncope," heat stroke, and dehydration. His sons, who would only recall having met him once before, were brought to his bedside. It is not known whether he received last rites from a priest—still less what he might have made of dying there, of all places. He was poor by then: he'd been cut off from the family fortune, his father's fortune, long before. I suppose that it was a small, cheap room near the attics, among the castellated chimneys and crocketed pinnacles and spires.

My conversion—now twenty years ago—was remarkably like Scott Junior's: less felt than arrived at as a necessary, logical, and inevitable destination. It was a kind of intellectual assent, enthusiastic to be sure, but I don't recollect much sense of freedom or peace: of mercy having befallen me and sins having been wiped away, of loving God and God loving me. Of his own conversion, Scott Junior said, "I experienced . . . no emotion, no surprise, I was not only cool but even cold." My own was similar. What I liked about religion was beauty, the form—the music, liturgy, architecture, and art—not the theological content. The form had a purpose, an essential one: to manifest the sacramental, the outward signs of inward, invisible, spiritual things, intimations of God that might be seen, heard, felt.

In London I had been attending church regularly, All Saints on Margaret Street near Oxford Circus. It was designed by William Butterfield and finished in 1859, the single modern church to gain Ruskin's praise as a worthy piece of architecture. That was enough for me, along with the church having been attended by Christina Rossetti and William Gladstone. Then as now the liturgy was as ornate and ritualistic as any in London, the choir a marvel, and the interior as beautiful as Ruskin had averred. Catholic or not, I might well have imagined that All Saints was visually and aurally more Catholic than the bulk of Roman churches. It aimed to inculcate the sacramental as few places could.

But it couldn't quite sustain my faith. The outward signs of interior, invisible things in my life were now manifest in Swinton Street, in Gissing's diaries, in Mrs. Ward's tortured doubters, not in this or any other church. Janey the Madwoman had recommended a novel, Rose Macaulay's *The Towers of Trebizond*. Macaulay was, in fact, an All Saints parishioner, which did not mean that she didn't see Anglo-Catholicism's potential shortcomings. In the novel (which itself mentions All Saints) the protagonist's aunt makes her realize that her faith is not much more than a taste for grandeur and ornament.

> "I think, my dear," she said, "the Church used once to be an opiate to you; a kind of euphoric drug. You dramatized it and yourself, you felt carried along in something aesthetically exciting and beautiful and romantic; you were a dilettante, escapist Anglican. I know you read Clement of Alexandria: do you remember where he says, 'We may not be taken up and transported to our journey's end, but must travel thither on foot, traversing the whole distance of the narrow way.' One mustn't lose sight of the hard core, which is, do this, do that,

love your friends and like your neighbors, be just, be extrav-
agantly generous, be honest, be tolerant, have courage, have
compassion, use your wits and your imagination, understand
the world you live in and be on terms with it, don't dramatize
and dream and escape."

Maybe that was why I'd come to London and lived among the
shades of the Victorians: to make the world more than ordinary,
to put myself into a drama where the imaginary was real and present reality was a blur, as in my photographs. Maybe God had been
an imaginary God, a product of my imagination; maybe I'd made
him up. And now that he'd slipped away, I would be Mrs. Ward's
Robert Elsmere, but without the nobility of purpose, the grasp
of Macaulay's "hard core." I'd be Gissing without all the labor, a
justified pessimist. As Macaulay's protagonist says, "Presently I
should come to it; already I was on the way. It would be a refuge,
that agnosticism into which I was slipping down." Maybe that
was what Janey, who'd recommended the book to me, had sensed:
that I, too, was coming into it; that I didn't seem to want anything.
Maybe she wasn't mad at all: maybe she saw right into me as I
could not; saw, too, where I was headed.

I hadn't been asking anything of the church except that it exist
and not change. I suppose that meant it could also be trusted not
to ask anything of me. It didn't occur to me that it might not be
so much about spectacle and tradition as about love, the promise that all shall be well, well with me. But I think when my life
took a turn toward unhappiness, toward suffering, that I had in
fact been hoping, however semiconsciously, for something like
that—call it grace—all along. When it didn't appear, I was bitter.
The promise was bogus: from that it followed that the ceremonies
and sacraments were hollow; they really were just theatre. So why
not exchange Newman's "assurance of things hoped for" for Gissing's "The Hope of Pessimism"? You might make something not
entirely unbearable out of it; you might even write a little now and
again.

One day every man turns around and sees that for all his struggles with being a son, despite himself, he's become a father or at least an old man. Scott Junior's sons came to him as he lay dying in his own father's masterwork. His life was concluded—he couldn't, as a son can, regard it as a work in progress that might be turned around or amended or justified. Now there would be a reckoning, a toting up of what must be regretted since it was too late to atone for. His sons stood at his bedside: he could be nothing in their presence but a father entombed in the encrustations and brick that his own father had built at the height of his powers. Did he say he was sorry?—and if he did, what would that have amounted to?

Of course, Scott Junior had already converted and presumably was still a believer on his deathbed. But he was unconscious when his sons reached him, so they wouldn't have the satisfaction of seeing him confess his sins as he took his last breath and perhaps feel their own resentments and wounds ease, if only a bit. Maybe they forgave him anyway, shamed him with their mercy, or—who can say?—allowed him to die at peace with himself. If nothing else, two of them became architects—and good ones, too.

What George Gissing did on his deathbed is slightly less of a mystery. He had settled in France in his final years, had an affectionate and devoted third wife, and was even having some financial and popular success with his most recent book, *The Private Papers of Henry Ryecroft*. But certainly his sons never saw him again. When he left England for the last time in 1901, he arranged for both of them to be boarded with relatives, feeling compunction but also relief. Of Alfred, the younger son, aged five, he wrote: "I always felt guilty of a crime in abandoning the poor little fellow. He will now have his chance to grow up in healthy and decent circumstances." His primary financial preoccupation would now be to save enough money to send them to good boarding schools. It never seemed to occur to him that they might benefit from his presence in their lives. Perhaps that's understandable in light of his self-loathing and the absence of a father in his own life. He might have asked himself: what would he have gotten from having a father? As for so many Victorian men, nothing much and perhaps worse.

Gissing was sick in those last years in France, ostensibly from tuberculosis but ultimately from his tertiary syphilis, moving from one supposedly health-giving resort to the next. But he was at long last content; had mustered as much happiness as he was capable of. He had acquired, if not celebrity, a solid standing as a "writer's writer" and had penetrated the inner social circle of Henry James, Joseph Conrad, Thomas Hardy (as much a pessimist as Gissing), and more. H. G. Wells was his closest writer friend and came to help tend him on his deathbed in St. Jean de Luze at Christmas in 1903.

Gissing and Wells were able to talk books and writing for a while. Then Gissing began hallucinating, telling his wife: "It is the light of the supernatural world. . . . It is unspeakably beautiful. And those voices singing in eternity! I see how foolish I was to doubt the existence of the supernatural." Wells thought Gissing had simply succumbed to dementia: " 'What are these magnificent beings!' [Gissing] would say. . . . Or again, 'What is all this splendour? What does it portend?' He babbled in Latin; he chanted fragments of Gregorian music."

The local Anglican priest, the Reverend Cooper, eager to substantiate the apparent deathbed conversion of a prominent agnostic, made much more of this. He claimed that Gissing was singing the "Te Deum" as he finally died on December 28. Cooper subsequently persuaded Gissing's wife to lay his body in repose before the altar of Cooper's church and to give him a full Anglican funeral.

Wells and Gissing's other writer friends were incredulous at the notion that he had undergone any sort of conscious conversion at the end, but many people were convinced otherwise. Within ten days of Gissing's death what would become a furious debate commenced with Cooper's assertion that Gissing "departed this life in God's faith & fear" and his account of Gissing's final days (at strong variance with that of Wells), in which his last words were "God's will be done." Cooper sent an identical account to the *Church Times*, the official newspaper of Anglicanism, which published it. The story was then refuted by Morley Roberts, Gissing's best friend, and by the deathbed nurse, who said that Cooper had not even been present during Gissing's final hours. Later H. G. Wells contributed a further explanation for Gissing's hallucinations and chanting: until a few days before his crisis, he had been immersed in research for what would have been a new novel, set in an Italian monastery. His widow could only say of his putative conversion: "Curious indeed considering G's anti-mystical leanings, his unqualified agnosticism, his lack of sympathy for any form of metaphysics."

A socialist, an existentialist, perhaps a nihilist: for a long while Gissing was one or all of these, but it's not impossible that he died some sort of believer. He was, more than any of these other identities, an Englishman who might have reached out for the English church if he couldn't die on English soil. Faith goes but can also return, sometimes more than once. Its departures could come as a relief or a devastation, its arrivals could be joyous but also unbidden, an uninvited guest who insists on staying despite all protest, all "difficulties."

Virginia Woolf and her friend Lytton Strachey were no kinder in death to Mrs. Humphry Ward than they had been when she was still writing: "She was merely a woman of straw after all—shoveled into the grave & already forgotten," Woolf commented. Ward had outlived the Victorian era by nineteen years, dying in 1920, publishing novels of less consequence and diminishing sales to the very end. By then her "free-thinking" and bluestocking do-gooding were obsolete, risible, not to say contemptible, to the new Bloomsbury set that had replaced hers. Her best-selling *Robert Elsmere* had made her a target, of course, and she'd been already parodied as "an ornament of intellectual Bloomsbury" in W. H. Mallock's popular satire *The Individualist*. But twenty years earlier, in 1878, Mallock had described her contemporaries as people "whose hearts are aching for the God they no longer believe in." In that, above all, they were the last Victorians: by the time Woolf and Strachey came of age the preoccupations that had roiled the world in 1888 and disturbed the prime minister himself were already moribund questions, the matter of belief not only settled but absurd.

But for me, even after reading Macaulay, Mrs. Ward's follow-up to *Elsmere*, *Hellbeck of Bennisdale*, was still compelling stuff. Her characters were wrestling with the same issues I had: whether they could remain or ought to become Catholic, especially when the faith's strictures seemed to be a bar to ordinary happiness. Ward had set those agonies in the Lake District (where her own family had its roots), like the early chapters of *Robert Elsmere*.

I found a literary guide to the Lakes with driving instructions to the places where Ward had set scenes in her novels, rented a car, and made a two-night reservation at a hotel, recommended as tranquil, welcoming, and with a good kitchen. I checked in at a desk manned by a diffident teenager, dropped off my bags, and headed out. Besides Ward, I wanted to visit locales associated with Gissing, the Brontës, Gaskell, and the younger Bloomsbury set. I had a lot of ground to cover.

I had settled on Longsleddale as the most representative Ward site, which featured in both *Elsmere* and *Hellbeck*. Leaving the highway, I bivouacked up a six-mile single track road into the hills, stopping and starting for vehicles coming in the other direction, for bridgeless stream crossings, and the ubiquitous sheep whose obliviousness to my car suggested that they were fearless or senseless. The six miles took a half hour.

The road ended in a rocky, boulder-strewn cirque with a few deserted stone barns and cottages a little way off. It wasn't what I had pictured. I'd imagined it as verdant and pastoral, but it was scoured and wind battered. The meadows were indeed covered in grass, but pale, blanched in a veiled light, less green than verdigris. I'd imagined copses and groves, not solitary trees, skeletal, surviving against the wind and gray in groups of two or three, ruins of what might once have been columns. I could hear but not see sheep: the flat bleat of dams, the higher-pitched, desolated cries of strayed lambs.

I'd brought color film. Later, when the proofs came back, it seemed at first glance that the shots were in black-and-white, the spectrum sucked into the hills, which might have been on the moon, mottled pewter. They were beautiful in the way that Ruskin would call sublime, "awful" in its literal sense. He would have seen the whole place charged with something that, if it was not God, was unimaginable, beyond our capacity to render not just with the eye in paint or pencil but with the mind, a register of being that humans could at best approximate, intuit by analogy, by a sketch of a rock-face, an emanation that you could only take in sidelong and from which you at times felt compelled to turn away.

Back at the hotel, the manager was waiting for me. I'd checked in for a two-night stay, but the hotel had a policy of a three-night minimum. I told her I had booked online and the website had allowed me that option; that I'd had no idea of the mandatory three-night policy. She looked at me askance, as though I were lying. I apologized for the confusion, adding, almost forlornly, that I had no other place to go, not at dusk, not in the misting rain. Her lips pursed, then she shrugged as though I must be incorrigible. She would let it go—this time. I sensed that I was going to be made to suffer for these two days.

At dinnertime I descended the stair, or rather skulked, afraid I'd run into her in reception or at the entrance to the dining room. I'd hoped for a table in the glassed conservatory that overlooked the valley below, a table with a view. But I imagined now that this might be denied me; that I was a second-class citizen in this place or something worse. I *should* have somehow noticed the three-night minimum, I thought to myself in one instant; then, in another, that she—who was no longer an individual woman but an archetype of the cold mother, wived to the authoritarian father—should not be so cruel, so unforgiving. It had been a mistake, not a sin.

I went out the next day and photographed the other places on my list. At dinner they gave me a table at the window, just as they had the night before. And happily—as though I'd gotten off scot-free, eluding the fear that she'd haunt me for the rest of my days—I never saw the manager again.

Chapter 4

MODERN TIMES

SOME DAYS on my walk toward St. Pancras and Bloomsbury, I'd descend through Granville Square, nearly hidden and approachable only through narrow streets at either side. The only egress in my direction was a set of steps, twenty in number, leading down to King's Cross Road and onward to Swinton Street. The steps form part of Gwynne Place (named for the pub across the street, itself named for Nell Gwynne, the seventeenth-century actress and courtesan), although it used to be known as Granville Place.

The novelist Arnold Bennett renamed them Riceyman Steps for the purposes of his 1923 novel of the same name. Beyond that alteration, Bennett stuck closely to the contours of the neighborhood, which had been my neighborhood for five months. I read the book eagerly. I'd come to love Finsbury, and the idea that a novelist of some renown had set a novel there resonated for me twice over. I was, so to speak, living inside Bennett's story and, being a novelist myself, could imagine his imagining it, his process, the ways in which he animated the characters that he had made from nothing and placed on these familiar streets.

Riceyman Steps both is and is not a Victorian novel, just as Bennett, who published his first book in 1898 and his last in 1931, both is and is not a Victorian writer. He was born into its traditions and conventions but outlived them by a quarter-century, keeping one foot in that world, putting the other in what would come to be called the modern world. *Riceyman Steps* partakes of both Dickens and Gissing: its protagonist, Henry Earlforward, has a dusty, anonymous used bookshop just below the steps, and he's a dusty, anonymous character, a sour prisoner of routines that he no longer remembers are of his own devising; a miser too, that most Victorian of pathologies, epitomized by *Our Mutual Friend*'s Golden Dustman and the legendary misers in the books he loves. The novel's other characters, in the High Victorian mode, include a hapless wife who doesn't know quite what to do about her husband and the bleak path he's taking them both down and a plucky young woman who thinks she does but can't save him from himself. Gissing is present in that, a step beyond Dickens: the pessimism about humans' capacity to alter their fate or improve themselves; what women can and cannot accomplish in an age of apparently changing gender roles; and the overarching presence of money or the want of it in every relationship.

But Bennett is also up to something new in *Riceyman Steps*, not perhaps "modern" in the way that the word will describe the Bloomsbury Group, but psychologically different from the Victorian novel and even epistemologically so. Henry does not so much have a defined character as he does a range of appearances, of possible but not settled traits: he "seems," "appears," and "might" be thought of in one way or another. Nor does he bother to examine or know himself or anyone else: "incurious of the mysteries in which [he] and all their fellows lived, Mr. Earlforward never asked the meaning of life, for he had a lifelong ruling passion." That passion is not immediately clear, but over the course of the

Gwynne Place. Photograph by author.

book, miserliness becomes its fullest expression. The miserliness is not the essence of Earlforward or even an affliction as it would be in a Victorian novel but a marker for some existential condition hidden so deeply that it can't be named: after losing a sixpence, he thinks: "Life was bigger, more cruel, more awful than he had imagined." By the end of the book, his miserliness has in concrete terms killed both him and his wife, but it has only been a means to an end; a suicide predicated on the refusal to truly exist.

The space just below the steps where the bookshop would have stood has changed a lot, the bulk of it occupied by a huge Travelodge hotel that straddles Gwynne Place with a second-story archway. Any traces of the nineteenth and early twentieth centuries have been obliterated. When I came by with my camera, no photographs suggested themselves. One day I saw a pile of junk against the south wall of the hotel, so I photographed that: a mattress, a bed frame, pieces of a wardrobe, a fuse panel, a plastic tray that might have been a cat box. A piece of the bed-frame hung tilted over the mattress, whose dust-ruffle was still attached, tumbling down in dirty folds of polyester. When I printed it, I thought this was the heart of the picture: the thing that rendered it almost but not quite beautiful.

Just above the hotel I could see the walls enclosing the still intact gardens of the Victorian houses in Granville Square, which were impoverished and squalid when Bennett wrote *Riceyman Steps*. He makes much mention of these walls, I suppose to remind us that Earlforward is hemmed in on all sides, a fate that he doesn't seem to mind a bit. Near the end of the novel there's a section about what happens on the other side of the walls, the side that Earlforward is barred from. The heretofore resourceful young woman Elsie, who has failed to save him, is looking out from an upstairs window.

> A lengthy perspective of the back-yards of the house stretched out before her; a pattern of dark walls—wall, yard, wall, yard, wall, yard—and joint masonries of every pair of dwellings jutting out at regular intervals. . . . Every upper window marked a bedroom. And in every bedroom were souls awake or asleep. Not a window lit, except one at the end of the vista. Perhaps behind that window someone was suffering and someone was watching. Or it might be only that someone was rising to an interminable, laborious day.

Like the rest of the novel, it's an "as if"/"what if" world, always provisional because always unknowable and of no interest anyway to the likes of Earlforward. But then something happens: a dog barks; a candle is lit; a beautiful woman appears and fills the concrete space in an unmistakable way:

> The woman advanced menacingly upon the young chained dog, and the next minute there was one sharp yell, followed by a diminuendo succession of yells: "That'll learn ye to keep people awake all night," Elsie heard a thin, inimical voice say. The woman returned to the house. The dog again began to yap and moan. The woman ran out in a fury, picked up the animal and

flung it savagely into the kennel. . . . The woman retired from her victory; the door was locked; the light showed once more at the bedroom window, and went out.

Bennett devoted the better part of two pages to this scene: in its length and apparent irrelevance to advancing the plot, it stands out, even jars, interrupting the pace and mood of the book. But I think that we're meant to pay attention, deep attention, to this breaking through of another reality, to the other side of those impenetrable, blank walls: meant to take it in and return to the novel, not quite knowing what to make of it.

Later, I looked at Bennett's notebook for *Riceyman Steps* in the New York Public Library. It has a black cover, veined with gold vine tendrils, and it is tiny, scarcely three by five inches. So is Bennett's handwriting, precise but for me unreadable without a magnifier. It reminded me of the notebooks that I'd kept for each of my own novels: words and phrases; odd bits of dialog; vital statistics and physical descriptions of the characters; the chronology and geography of the novel's incidents and scenes.

Bennett had drawn a map of Granville Square and the steps, just as I would have done. On the inside cover he wrote down the points he wanted to keep in mind:

more intimate psychology
grand passion
heroic plane
spiritual grandeur of all three

The last entry must refer to Earlforward, his wife, and Elsie. Reading the finished book, it seems an odd intent for Bennett to have had. There's no grandeur in any of them, it seemed to me, and still less of the spiritual. The "intimate psychology" I could see; the "heroic plane" not at all. The "grand passion" must be Earlforward's miserliness, as though he has set himself to becoming the greatest miser imaginable. I wasn't allowing for irony, though: for the thought that miserliness doesn't extend toward grandeur but shrinks, compacting generosity and abundance down to nothing at all.

What I mainly noticed in the notebook were single words, freestanding and disconnected, though some were repeated: "greed," for example, and "neighbours over the wall." There were lists of characteristics, chiefly of Earlforward:

Eternal delusion
His extreme detachment
Lavish in his self-selfishness
Remember that he confused love and dream

But there were mostly things:

Bacon
Cake
Braces
Tears
Relics
Jam on table

And then, near the last page, "Cruel Things."

I wondered if I would have liked a bookshop like Earlforward's; if I might like his life. Not the self-imposed penury, but its willful interment within its own walls, its obliviousness to the cruel things undergone by others, its "self-selfishness," by which I imagine Bennett meant something like narcissism, a refusal to extend beyond yourself.

That seems to me a harsh judgment to make about myself. But it replicates a very Victorian cast of mind; to take doubt and a sense of failure and press them to a logical extreme: not to shame or guilt, because these depend on a sense of sin that no longer obtains, but to a position of utter defeat that might not be much different from nihilism. In that defeat you do indeed see over a wall to the cruel things undergone by people you've never seen, but you are helpless to do anything about any of it— a condition that is no longer Victorian but, it feels to me, modern.

The moderns themselves would not have agreed with me: Virginia Woolf was scarcely kinder to Bennett than she was to Mrs. Ward. For her, his books were retrograde and he was a comical figure. He came to tea more than a few times at the houses of Woolf and her friends; after he left, they mocked him. He wanted to be modern, to get the approval of this new generation, which only rendered him more ridiculous. He didn't grasp what was up: he was neither here nor there.

Leslie Stephen was a kind of ultimate late Victorian man of letters: vastly industrious, the author of twenty books and editor of the 63-volume *Dictionary of National Biography,* a scholarly monument equal to *The Oxford English Dictionary,* one of those feats of sheer accumulative, tireless pack-rattery that the Victorians were so drawn to. He was also a prominent agnostic and an avid mountaineer. He was married twice: first to Thackeray's daughter, Minny, and, after her early death, to Julia Duckworth, a daughter of the Holland Park Circle of artists and upper-class bohemians, including Edward Burne-Jones, G. F. Watts, and, notably, Holman Hunt, who proposed marriage to her and was refused, though he did persuade her to model for his painting *The Lady of Shalott.*

Julia Duckworth accepted the proposal from Stephen—seemingly less attractive, wealthy, and prepossessing than her other suitors—who adored her. She was, in lieu of God and church, his redemption: "You see," he wrote her after their engagement, "I have not got any saints and you must not be angry if I put you in the place where my saints ought to be." She tolerated his adoration—she was a level-headed woman and, though beautiful, without vanity—and his other aspects; he was not an easy man to live with, given his obsessive-compulsive streak, his perfectionism, and his incessant labor. There was also a strain of madness in his blood, a tendency to disassociation, perhaps exacerbated by too much study, too much thinking. He might have been following in the footsteps of his father, who had written:

I am sometimes oppressed by myself. I seem to come too closely in contact with myself. It is like the presence of an unwelcome visitor. . . . Yet I suppose everyone has now and then felt as if he were two persons in one, and were compelled to hold a discourse in which soliloquy and colloquy mingled oddly and awfully.

Stephen's cousin Jem, like George Gilbert Scott Junior, had been committed to Northhampton, and Stephen himself had contemplated suicide. Following the trajectory of *Robert Elsmere*, he had taken holy orders as a priest after college and then realized not long after that he was, in fact, an agnostic. But his ensuing suicidal despair was prompted not only by his loss of faith but just as much by his shame and sense of being a failure. Looking back on his life, he perceived "how little I have done," judging himself at best "a jack of all trades," a footnote in the "history of English thought in the nineteenth century." Thomas Hardy, who had been a witness to Stephen's collapse upon resigning the priesthood, later concluded, "I have always felt that a tragic atmosphere encircled Leslie Stephen's history and was suggested in some indefinable way by his presence." There was something spectral about Stephen, a kind of death in life, a mournful, morbid aspect that neither work nor intellect could lighten.

Despite that, he would not brook self-pity or even sentimentality, which he defined as "when we make a luxury of grief and regard sympathetic emotion as an end rather than a means." Beneath the driving, imperial public ethos of Victorian life ran a current of despair, of implacable loss, a dangerous feeling that had to be displaced with more something more bearable, less shaming and helpless, that could be dealt with by a show of right feeling and high moral tone. Stephen's daughter Virginia would write of her mother's generation: "Tragedies were the breath of their nostrils. Some small boy died of an operation. That was delightful. Then 'unselfishness' was at a premium."

But Stephen inspired love and devotion. In *To the Lighthouse*, Virginia would say of the character modeled on her father, "No one attracted her more; his hands were beautiful to her and his feet and his voice, and his words and his haste, and his temper and his oddity, and his passion, and his remoteness. . . . 'Do this,' 'Do that'; his dominance; his 'Submit to me.' "

The way Stephen educated Virginia and her sister Vanessa reflected these qualities. By then Oxford and Cambridge had women's colleges (among them Somerville, founded by Mrs. Humphry Ward among others), but he preferred to take matters in hand himself. (The girls' two brothers, of course, were sent to boarding schools.) When Virginia was fifteen, he assigned the following texts: James Anthony Froude, *Thomas Carlyle*; Mandell Creighton, *Queen Elizabeth*; James Stephen, *Essays in Ecclesiastical Biography*; J. Dykes Campbell, *Samuel Taylor Coleridge: A Narrative of the Events of His Life*; J. R. Lowell, *Poems*; Thomas Carlyle, *Life of John Sterling*; Samuel Pepys, *Diary*; Thomas Macaulay, *History of England*; Carlyle, *French Revolution*; Carlyle, *Oliver Cromwell's Letters and Speeches*; Thomas Arnold, *History of Rome*; Froude, *History of England*; and his own *Life of Fawcett*. Stephen expected these would be fully digested and then regurgitated in his top floor study at 22 Hyde Park Gate. Virginia—as untiring a worker as her father—did that and more. She and Vanessa produced a household newspaper, painted and drew (Vanessa would become a formidable artist), and, with Julia, mastered the Victorian curriculum of women's duties. The house sat a few blocks from the Albert Memorial: "eleven people aged between eight and sixty lived there, and were waited upon by seven servants, while various old women and lame men did odd jobs with rakes and pails by day." Virginia would remember 22 Hyde Park Gate as an immense cabinet of Victoriana:

One never knew when one rummaged in the many dark cupboards whether one would disinter Herbert Duckworth's barrister's wig, my father's clerical collar, or a sheet scribbled over with drawings by Thackeray. . . . Old letters filled dozens of black tin boxes. One opened them and got a terrific whiff of the past. There were chests of heavy family plate. There were hoards of china and glass.

She would not have said that this amounted to a "happy childhood"—Virginia was as wary of sentimentality as her father—but it was perhaps an interesting one. Looking back, she'd say, "It seems a morbid life now; choked with draperies and ornaments."

Death would visit Virginia and Vanessa often and early: Julia died in 1895 when Virginia was thirteen, and it devastated the household, but no one more than Stephen. With much the same dogged resolution that he brought to *The National Dictionary of Biography*, he began compiling what he called *The Mausoleum Book*, where he wrote endlessly of Julia and then of any and all friends who died until he himself died, nine years after Julia, in 1904. Did he "make a luxury of grief," his onetime definition of sentimentality, or was it something more: "awful" in some deeply Ruskinian way, a confrontation with the terror of death, against which Victorian high-mindedness and industry were powerless?

The Mausoleum Book, Stephen always maintained, was a book for his children. He dictated its final passage to Virginia on his deathbed: "I shall write no more in this book. . . . I have only to say to you, my children, that you have all been as good and tender to me as anyone could be during these last months and indeed years. It comforts me to think you are so fond of each other that when I am gone you are better able to do without me."

They did not do well, especially Virginia. She was immune to sentimentality, an anti-Victorian in so many ways just as her father was, in his ways, the arch-Victorian. But she could not evade his generation's congenital malady, the curse of manic, near fathomless grieving, depthless as its dead God. She spent the year of his death in madness and made her first suicide attempt, stepping out of a window.

Maybe that summer of 1904 was when the Victorian age ended for Virginia rather than with the death of Victoria herself in 1901. Or perhaps it was the year before, the year of her "coming out" into society, when Virginia had seen Holman Hunt, her mother's erstwhile suitor, for the last time. Virginia had known him since she was a girl: the Hunts (Holman married one of his models, Edith Waugh) vacationed in Cornwall in the same town as the Stephens, and their son Hillary was a close friend of her brother Thoby.

But it was a night in 1903 that Virginia remembered most, and she wrote about it twice over. Escorted by her half-brother George Duckworth, she dined with Lady Carnarvon and her friend Mrs. Popham of Littlecote. After asking the former if she had read the dialogues of Plato, Virginia realized that "I had committed some unspeakable impropriety." George whispered to her, "They're not used to young women saying *anything*." She left, chastened by what her father's instruction about the world had left out. Though she expected they'd go home, the carriage took her and George to the Hunts at 18 Melbury Road, Kensington. "I think you want a little practice in how to behave to strangers," George said.

The street was packed with carriages and broughams, and inside she recognized William Morris's widow and daughters as well Edward Burne-Jones. As she later recorded, they went into the studio:

There we found old Holman Hunt dressed in a long Jaeger dressing gown, holding forth to a large gathering about the ideas that had inspired him in painting "The Light of the World," a copy of which stood upon the easel. He sipped cocoa and stroked his flowing beard as he talked, and we sipped cocoa and shifted our shawls—for the room was chilly—as we listened. Occasionally some of us strayed off to examine with reverent murmurs other bright pictures upon other easels, but the tone of the assembly was devout, high-minded, and to me after the tremendous experiences of the evening, sooth-ingly and almost childishly simple. George was never lack-ing in respect for old men of recognised genius, and now he advanced with his opera hat pressed beneath his arm; drew his feet together, and made a profound bow over Holman Hunt's hand. Holman Hunt had no notion of who he was, or indeed who any of us were; but went on sipping his cocoa, stroking his beard, and explaining what ideas had inspired him in painting "The Light of the World," until we left.

Virginia would say that George lived in 1860 while she and Vanessa "were living in, say, 1910." Maybe that was the source of his obeisance to the great Victorian and his greatest painting; maybe it even had something to do with what he did when he and Virginia got home and she went to her room:

I stood slipping off my petticoats, withdrew my long white gloves, and hung my white silk stockings over the back of a chair. Many different things were whirling round in my mind—diamonds and countesses, copulations, the dialogues of Plato . . . and "The Light of the World." Ah, how pleasant it would be to stretch out in bed, fall asleep and forget them all!

Sleep had almost come to me. The room was dark. The house was silent. Then, creaking stealthily; treading gingerly, someone entered. "Who?" I cried. "Don't be frightened," George whispered. "And don't turn on the light, oh beloved. Beloved"—and he flung himself on my bed, and took me in his arms.

Yes, the old ladies of Kensington and Belgravia never knew that George Duckworth was not only father and mother, brother and sister to those poor Stephen girls; he was their lover also.

The word "lover" was, if not an evasion, a euphemism; a stay, maybe, against rage and grieving. Someone had come to Virginia's door, not knocking; not her savior, but her rapist. She would say later that it had been "to comfort me for the fatal illness of my father—who was dying three or four storeys lower down of cancer."

I gave up grieving when I was nine. I remember the exact moment. My mother and stepfather sat me and my sister down and announced that they were getting divorced. My mother's first divorce had transpired when I was two, my father had died when I was seven, and this latest rupture seemed of a piece with these others. This is the way life is and ever shall be, I remember feeling. And then I swore something like a pledge to myself: I am not going to let this touch me or anything else of the kind, ever again.

What I swore off, I think, was the incorporation of loss into my life: I simply refused to engage with it—no grieving, no tears, no impossible longing for what or who was no more. I didn't go to funerals unless compelled to; didn't rage against or mourn deaths that came close by; I "moved on" without so much as a pause; achieved closure because I had never been open to loss in the first place.

In that regard, my obsession with Victoriana was scarcely incongruent, for the Victorians were nothing if not history's most exquisite and accomplished mourners. As befit an empire, Victorian mourning knew no bounds and bestowed on grieving a kind of pomp, the status of religion, state, monarchy. A huge industry grew up to supply mourning dress and ceremonials; the pioneers of photography applied themselves to shooting portraits of corpses; Tennyson, the poet-laureate, wrote his masterpiece and called it "In Memoriam." Spiritualists and mediums conversed with the dead at seances attended by some of the brightest, most rational people in Victorian society. Loss was infinite—no God was going to stanch it—and had no end except in becoming lost yourself, in grief as the way, the truth, and the life; in failure, madness, and maniacal labor and striving.

In sum, that was Leslie Stephen too, whose daughter Virginia became an astute analyst of loss and, concomitantly, of the Victorian age. In one of her voluminous notebooks and journals—like her father, she typically worked fourteen or fifteen hours a day—she created a selective chronology of its whole span:

1882: Ireland bombs. Parnell. 1883: women's property act. Missing link at aquarium. Thought reading and table turning looked into. Ballooning. 1885: Fall of Khartoum. Fabian society founded. A summer of most unusual heat—90 in the shade. 1886: Gladstone comes in—Question of Home Rule. The riot in Trafalgar Square. Dogs muzzled. Fencing taken up by women. Newspapers largely occupied with celebration of Queens [sic] Jubilee. 1888: The union of match girls. Parachutes from balloons. Electric light in home to home scheme. Phonograph. Jack the Ripper. 1890: Parnell. Tate Gallery projected. Gambling by working men. O'Shea case. 1891: The split over Parnell in the Irish Party. Influenza. Man who broke the bank. White man's burden—Kipling. Death of Parnell. 1892: Tararaboomdeeay. Tendency of average man to make more of his own interests. Oscar Wilde. Barrie. Tess. Paderewski. Women's suffrage defeated. 1893: Why educate workmen. Home Rule Bill. Second Mrs. Tanqueray. Modern girl: bicycles, lawn tennis. The Boer War. Oscar Wilde downfall. Cycling allowed in Hyde Park. 1896: Dr. Jameson raid. Incandescent gas—craze for bicycles. 1898: Dreyfus. 1899: The weekend habit. Tremendous entertaining. Womens [sic] extravagance. Women for the first time bought papers in the street. 1900: People broke laurel leaves from the Queens [sic] wreaths at her funeral.

She dealt in the subjective and whimsical as much as in great men and deeds, but her list is also an implicit history of the progress of women. Virginia—now surnamed Woolf and a resident of Bloomsbury—sensed that the whole era was in an unacknowledged but fundamental way about women; that women from Victoria down to her mother's guests at tea manifested both its essence and its posterity:

Like cows uneasily aware of a thunderstorm . . . the mother feeling her office in danger; feeling society coming to an end. . . . So history will see these Victorian mothers doomed; but fighting—under a cloud of ignorance. They could not foretell 1914, let alone Hitler. But looking back I think they had premonitions; and that they grasped teapots so hard because they were to be smashed.

That was the view from Bloomsbury, where so much of what was forbidden by her parent's generation was permitted, even celebrated. And in a strange way the parents had made it all possible. Francis Birrell, a gay novelist, once wrote to Virginia about her father: "He made it possible for me to have a decent life. He pulled down the whole edifice, & never knew what he was doing. He never realised that if God went, [conventional] morality must follow." Virginia saw that the stage had been set and the future enacted: "There is no Shakespeare, there is no Beethoven; certainly and emphatically there is no God; we are the words, we are the music, we are the thing itself." So much for grieving, for the Albert Memorial, for the mausoleum.

If her father's time had not ended by 1904, the year of his death, it had surely ended by 1910, the year Holman Hunt died. Virginia famously decreed that "in or about December, 1910, human character changed." I am not sure why she chose that particular date, but the sentence rings ominously: nothing was or ever will be the same, it implies. "All human relations have shifted," she said, "those between masters and servants, husbands and wives, parents and children. And when human relations change there is at the same time a change in religion, conduct, politics, and literature."

Practically speaking, 1910 was the year Edward VII died: Victoria's wayward, dissolute son, whose pointless monarchy marked the languid fizzle of his mother's and her time. Woolf's remark has specifically to do with the state of the novel and the firm line that she wanted to draw between Edwardian novelists and her own generation, whom she calls "Georgian," after the new king. She meant to plant the flag of what came to be called modernism and announce that hereafter writing and art would go forward in a strikingly different way.

In the essay titled "Mr. Bennett and Mrs. Brown," Virginia names a rogue's gallery of Edwardian novelists to set against the Georgians: H. G. Wells, John Galsworthy, and especially Arnold Bennett versus E. M. Forster, D. H. Lawrence, James Joyce, T. S. Eliot, and the Bloomsbury historical biographer Lytton Strachey. But it was Bennett who was her whipping boy, whom she disparaged and mocked both in print and in conversation.

Myself, I loved his novel *Riceyman Steps.* On my daily walks it was an anchor, the steps themselves a sort of correlative to my writing life, to the business of turning experience into art. The fictional Riceyman Steps, as Bennett called them, had a real life counterpart in Gwynne Place, steps I could descend and ascend: one foot in the world of imagination, in the novelist's fabricated transfiguration of life and fact, the other in actuality. I didn't want to give them up in order to be in harmony with Woolf. They meant something that I hadn't yet put my finger on; something to do with transiting the distance from my flat and Gissing's misery and then my panic in Swinton Street to a place beyond them, a Bloomsbury where there was clarity, a sense of vocation; maybe of being at home in the present. But, in that interim at least, I couldn't take the step beyond those things into Bloomsbury. Maybe it was in truth a sentimental attachment, an evasion of loss and true feeling as Stephen would have it, but sentiment would have to do until I could locate the other thing, whatever it might be.

Woolf's chief criticism of Bennett rested on his reliance on external, mostly inanimate detail to imply internal mental states and feelings: the way, say, Elsie's view onto the courtyard and the beating of the dog reflect the state of things for her and for everyone at the end of *Riceyman Steps*. It said all that—*meant* all that—for me, but for Woolf it was an artistic cheat, a lazy evasion of

Riceyman Steps (Gwynne Place). Photograph by author.

doing the writer's true work that asked the reader to do it instead: "Mr. Bennett . . . is trying to make us imagine for him; he is trying to hypnotize us into the belief that, because he has made a house, there must be a person living there."

I especially didn't like Woolf's attack on Bennett's plentiful descriptions of bricks and mortar, roads and trains, life's externals, its topmost fabric. I felt accused: me with my dozens of photos of walls, doors, streets, and steps (I had two dozen shots of Gwynne Place), all unpeopled except when the people were blurred. Was I a cheat, my work dishonest, someone who couldn't face real feeling or the world as it truly is? Was I a sentimentalist, unable to cope with or acknowledge loss, thus immersed in the past, the past now failing me, failing to keep the present at bay? I feared so—and now, looking back from here, from the present, I think so.

Virginia Stephen, like her mother, had marriage proposals she couldn't accept. The one she received in 1909 was from Lytton Strachey, among the most flamboyant members of Cambridge's archhomosexual Apostles club—he "corrupted Cambridge as Socrates corrupted Athens," his friend Leonard Woolf would say. Strachey was sincere, though; he had already had and would have sexual relationships with women, but they always ended in deep friendship, in devoted *marriages blancs*. That was the turn that his and Virginia's relationship took, too, and she would marry Leonard Woolf three years later. Next to Virginia herself, Strachey probably had the most acute mind in Bloomsbury and certainly the drollest. He, too, had grown up by Hyde Park, on the northern, opposite side, also in a tall, cluttered house, not as bookish as hers, neither as interesting nor, in its peculiar way, as happy. But it was just as Victorian, more so in some ways: aristocratic on his mother's side, well established in the Indian Colonial Service on his father's. The rooms were high-ceilinged and large windowed but shadowy. He was sent to a boarding school whose motto was "Education Spells Empire"; his family expected him to become a high-level civil servant, a gentleman who would be powerful but leisured enough to avoid seeming to be "in trade." But it was Strachey who would in many ways bring the Victorian era to a close, finish it off and bury it, not through history but through a new kind of biographical essay that could express or at least suggest, as in Woolf's manifesto, the inner life of its characters, truths that went beyond facts into the heart of things.

That was something Strachey had been thinking about for a long while. "We are all cupboards with obvious outsides," he wrote a friend in 1902, just down from Cambridge, "which may be either beautiful or ugly, simple or elaborate, interesting or unamusing—but with insides mysteriously all the same—the abodes of darkness, terror and skeletons." He would make it his business to look into the cupboards, to see people naked: not just individuals, but the world he'd grown up in. That same year he had a fantasy of people of his parents' generation passing by the Albert Memorial:

Suppose their astonished eyes were to perceive that the imposing golden form was no longer in a sitting posture, but had risen to its feet. . . . Imagine they saw too that it had discarded that princely robe, those knee-breeches, those stockings which we have all admired so, that it stood there in the garb of nature. . . . Imagine this, and imagine the accumulated force of horror and disgust and fury in the breasts of the passers-by. Imagine the indignant rush up those sacred steps, the blind fingers tearing, overturning, destroying . . . but to contemplate our late beloved Prince in such a situation is too painful; I draw a shuddering veil.

Those last phrases were in Strachey's facetious, proto-camp mode, his way of saying offhand things that were, in fact, meant to be disturbing; he wanted, Woolf would say, "to deal little words that poison vast monsters of falsehood." He had created a style, Wildean but more corrosive, that seemed to go with his body: angular, frail, with impossibly long fingers and an attenuated, high voice pitched for mockery. He'd also begun to find his great subject, the Victorians.

What an appalling time to have lived. It was the Glass Case Age. Themselves as well as their ornaments, were left under glass cases. Their refusal to face any fundamental question fairly—either about people or God— . . . was simply the result of an innate incapacity for penetration—for getting either out of themselves or into anything or anyone else. . . . Have you noticed they were nearly all physically impotent?—Matthew Arnold, Jowett, Leighton, Ruskin, Watts. It's damned difficult to copulate through a glass case.

But Strachey knew, too, how to take the Victorians seriously, to draw a hard, contrasting line between the generations: "We are greater than our fathers. . . . We have abolished religion, we have founded ethics, we have established philosophy, we have sown our strange illumination in every province of thought, we have conquered art, we have liberated love." It was a large, pretentious claim, and he allowed that it might take a while to be self-evident: "Our time will come in about a hundred years hence." That was in 1906: sixty-some years on, when I was Strachey's age, I imagined the same thing about my generation. Now it's more than 110 years since he made the remark and I am much less sure; certainly about my own generation, which has perhaps found a glass case of its own—an enclave of unacknowledged privilege where irony hides our failed expectations, half-buried self-pity. As for his— yes, maybe they did, for a while, achieve such things in Bloomsbury; and then the case slammed shut once more.

Strachey got the idea for a book around the time Woolf said that human character had changed, in 1911: he'd write a set of impressionistic biographical essays on "eminent Victorians," which would also be the book's title. "They seem to me a set of mouthing bungling hypocrites; but perhaps really there is a baroque charm about them which will be discovered by our great-grandchildren."

That, I have thought, could be me: by chronology, I could be one of those great-grandchildren. He chose four people to write about: Cardinal Henry Edward Manning, leader of the renascent Catholic church in England and builder of Westminster Cathedral; Florence Nightingale, the Crimean War's "Lady of the Lamp" and founder of modern nursing; Thomas Arnold, headmaster of Rugby School (and uncle of Mrs. Humphry Ward); and General Charles George Gordon, hero and martyr of the Siege of Khartoum. "They are, in one sense, haphazard visions—that is to say, my choice of subjects has been determined by no desire to construct a system or to prove a theory, but by simple motives of convenience and of art. It has been my purpose to illustrate rather than to explain."

Strachey was a thorough and meticulous researcher. He spent six years on the project, the years of World War I, working at his mother's house in Belsize Park Gardens in London and in several country cottages. It has been said that the research seems a little too meticulous; that he can't have known what he purports to know. Here is Cardinal Manning:

> When the guests were gone, and the great room was empty, the old man would draw himself nearer to the enormous fire, and review once more, for the thousandth time, the long adventure of his life. He would bring out his diaries and his memoranda, he would rearrange his notes, he would turn over again the yellow leaves of faded correspondences. . . . He would snip with scissors the pages of ancient journals, and with delicate ecclesiastical fingers, drop unknown mysteries into the flames.
>
> Sometimes he would turn to the four red folio scrapbooks with their collection of newspaper cuttings, concerning himself, over a period of thirty years. Then the pale cheeks would flush and the close-drawn lips would grow even more menacing than before. "Stupid, mulish malice," he would note. "Pure lying—conscious, deliberate and designed." "Suggestive lying."

It is perhaps too strong a term, but that last phrase may not be too far from what Strachey flirts with in such passages—or, rather, his style does. It's style that takes me in, that seduces me; that inculcates a sense of a truth being told that's truer than verifiable fact. "Uninterpreted truth," he'd said, "is as useless as burned gold, and art is the great interpreter."

As for malice, again, a case can be made. But, again, it's moderated by the style, which suggests rather than asserts, which raises questions without answering them explicitly but leaves the reader always attuned to irony, bad faith, and what Strachey and Woolf called "humbug." The author and his style have made us "insiders"—privy to what the subject of the essay and his contemporaries were not—so we're inclined to believe him; the style flatters us.

Perhaps when I first read *Eminent Victorians* I was sensitive in this area, still of two minds about my faith. But the one thing it is openly hostile toward is religion. Manning is portrayed as ambitious, Nightingale as neurotic and manipulative, Arnold as dense, and Gordon as suicidally barmy. What they all have in common is religious faith, seemingly fanatical faith rooted in childhood evangelicalism and credulity. Of Manning's fellow convert, Newman, Strachey says, "When Newman was a child he 'wished that he could believe the Arabian Nights were true.' When he came to be a man, his wish seems to have been granted." As for the institutional church: "If the Pope were indeed nothing more than a magnified Borough Councillor, we should hardly have heard so much of him. It is not because he satisfies the reason, but because he astounds it, that men abase themselves before the Vicar of Christ." And Manning's mentor, John Keble, is shown to be an advocate of universal ignorance: " 'It would be a gain to this country,' Keble observed, 'were it vastly more superstitious, more bigoted, more gloomy, more fierce in its religion, than at present it shows itself to be.' "

In Nightingale's case, her religion is both ostentatiously scrupulous and self-serving, used to further her ambitions as a would-be saintly busybody: "It was in vain that she prayed to be delivered from vanity and hypocrisy, and she could not bear to smile or to be gay, 'because she hated God to hear her laugh, as if she had not repented of her sin.' " General Gordon, though a theological crackpot, is the one figure in *Eminent Victorians* for whom Strachey seems to have had some imaginative sympathy, conjuring up "the light, gliding figure, and the blue eyes with the candor of childhood still shining in them; one can almost hear the low voice, the singularly distinct articulation, the persuasive—the self-persuasive—sentences, following each other so unassumingly between the puffs of a cigarette." Strachey's account of Gordon also seems to be the most historiographically credible of the four essays. Gordon had been sent on the authority of Sir Evelyn Baring—the villain of the piece—to protect British interests in Sudan with no practicable plans to provide reinforcements should he need them. Khartoum was, in the event, overrun; Gordon was killed, the last man standing. Strachey accepts that view and moreover portrays him as an enemy of humbug, quoting his diary approvingly:

I dwell on the joy of never seeing Great Britain again, with its horrid, wearisome dinner-parties and miseries. How we can put up with those things, passes my imagination! It is a perfect bondage . . . I would sooner live like a Dervish with the Mahdi, than go out to dinner every night in London.

It sounds remarkably like Strachey himself. Gordon died, so legend quickly had it, with that English aplomb typified by Captain Titus Oates of Robert Falcon Scott's Antarctic Expedition, who sacrificed himself, saying, "I am just going outside and may be some time." In this case, Strachey seems to have believed and confirmed the legend. His Gordon dies with a kind of wry shrug, resigned to the stupidity and poor manners of foreigners. His last known conversation (with a supplier of materiel) is reported by Strachey as follows:

"What more can I say?" he exclaimed, in a voice such as the merchant had never heard before. "The people will no longer believe me. I have told them over and over again that help would be here, but it has never come, and now they must see I tell them lies. I can do nothing more. Go, and collect all the people you can on the lines, and make a good stand. Now leave me to smoke these cigarettes."

Eminent Victorians ends with Gordon's funeral. Strachey's tone is still sardonic and religion still the font of hypocrisy and ignorance, but with a measured fury that sums up the book's case against the Victorians, against the glass case and its Bennett-like refusal to encounter the inner life, "the abodes of darkness, terror and skeletons," against the world they had made and what it had wrought:

> It was thought proper that a religious ceremony in honour of General Gordon should be held at the palace at Khartoum . . . and concluded with a performance of "Abide with Me"—the General's favourite hymn—by a select company of Sudanese buglers. Everyone agreed that General Gordon had been avenged at last. . . . But General Gordon had always been a contradictious person—even a little off his head, perhaps, though a hero; and besides, he was no longer there to contradict. . . . At any rate, it had all ended very happily—in a glorious slaughter of 20,000 Arabs, a vast addition to the British Empire, and a step in the Peerage for Sir Evelyn Baring.

Still, I think Strachey felt pity as well. When he had begun the project six years earlier, he'd marveled at the Victorians' "brave concealment of tragedy! . . . What a world, what a life, passing in these dimnesses." He was aware, too, that he was inevitably the son of his father and his age and that "to reconstruct, however dimly, that grim machine, would be to realize . . . the essential substance of my biography." That came, perhaps, from Strachey's knowledge of Freud; his brother, James Strachey, was one of the founders of psychoanalysis in Britain. Freud himself would read *Eminent Victorians*, seeing it as essentially a treatise against religion. Lytton knew about the inexorable return of the repressed; the way what is buried must erupt into the light, often explosively.

Published a few months before Armistice Day in 1918, *Eminent Victorians* was a sensation, both for its irreverence and iconoclasm and as a thrilling departure in historical storytelling. It was, more astonishingly, a best seller—90,000 copies—in wartime, when, for the first two-thirds, at least, attitudes other than cheery optimism were deeply suspect. But by 1918—"How long will this madness last?" Strachey was forever writing to friends—much of the public had moved on from early enthusiasm for the war to appalled inurement. Strachey and most of his Bloomsbury acquaintances had been in that state of mind from the start. Strachey joined two different anticonscription societies and went before a tribunal to defend his conscientious objector status. Young men were dying in flocks, by the thousands, in the government-sanctioned massacres of the Somme and Ypres. Rupert Brooke, whom both Lytton and James had been in love with, was killed one year into the war. It then seemed to Lytton that resistance was meaningless; that meaning itself was meaningless; that even nihilism amounted to less than nothing: "The meaninglessness of Fate is intolerable; it's all muddle and futility. After all the pother of those years living, to effect—simply nothing. It is like a confused tale, just beginning and then broken off for no reason, and forever. One hardly knows whether to be sorry even."

By the time Strachey got to the Florence Nightingale chapter at the beginning of 1915, that was the context of *Eminent Victorians*, infecting the entire enterprise. What marked the end of the Victorian age? Not the death of the queen in 1901, not December 1910, but this war. What caused the war? "The Glass Case," the "brave concealment of tragedy," the evasions, the distraction and self-justification of empire, willed blindness replacing faith. *Eminent Victorians* never openly said this; it went without saying. I had come to see it myself.

One of Strachey's Bloomsbury crushes, David Garnett, put it plainly: "Lytton's essays were designed to undermine the foundations on which the age that brought war about had been built." No less than the archpropagandist of empire saw it too: "I've been reading *Eminent Victorians*," Rudyard Kipling wrote. "It seems to me downright wicked in its heart." That attack would have gratified Strachey hugely. By and large, though, he could not escape praise for the book, even from the people who ought to have been appalled: the ones Bloomsbury was appalled by. He was feted, not least, by Arnold Bennett, who kept a copy on his parlor table, "constantly *en lecture.*"

Strachey had spent the war writing *Eminent Victorians* and by its end could also justify his claim of 1904 that "we have liberated love," at least for himself, his friends, and his lovers. He cast his net widely, among both men and women, though it is hard to know which attractions were crushes and which were consummated. Women were a more theoretical interest. He proposed marriage to Virginia Woolf not because he was in love with her in any erotic sense but because the intensity of their developing friendship during 1909 made the next step seem inevitable. But "as I did it, I saw it would be death if she accepted me. . . . I was in terror lest she should kiss me." She did accept him, but both of them quickly came to their senses.

In the throes of writing his Thomas Arnold chapter, Strachey did something similar on meeting the painter Dora Carrington in 1915, embracing and kissing her passionately on a country walk. Carrington was shocked and puzzled, not least when a friend explained that Strachey was homosexual: "What's that?" Carrington responded. Strachey would tell her himself and apologize for his impulsive gesture, but by that time Carrington was already in love with him and would never love anyone else as profoundly.

To look at photographs of her today, she seems a tomboyish, essentially plain woman indifferent to fashion and grooming, whose behavior was capricious and eccentric. But handsome, gifted men fell in love with her and pursued her despite her wild swings of interest or lack thereof: Mark Gertler, the painter; Gerald Brennan, the writer; and Ralph Partridge, one of Lytton's most fervid crushes. It was Ralph that she finally married, though not before giving up her virginity to Lytton, which he appears to have agreed to out of something like kindness. The marriage to Ralph was more *blanc* than not, though he and Gerald Brennan would continue to compete for her attention for years afterward. Still, she would live with Lytton for the next sixteen years—Partridge and Brennan entering and exiting—until Lytton's death, after which she committed suicide.

Although Lytton would sigh in mock befuddlement—"the world is rather tiresome, I must say—everything at sixes and sevens—ladies in love with buggers and buggers in love with woman-isers"—it was a circus in which he seemed willing to serve as ring-master. Maybe, having made a religion of art, he aimed to make a religion of love, to establish and inculcate what he'd been call-ing since Cambridge "the Higher Sodomy." It was an experiment whose form spread outward to involve family and friends too, even if not sexually. By 1919, on just one side of Gordon Square, the painter Duncan Grant and his lover, Vanessa Bell, Virginia's sis-ter, were at number 37; Lytton's brother James and his wife, Alix, at number 41; Lytton's other brother, Oliver, at number 42; Vir-ginia and Vanessa's brother Adrian and his wife, Karin, at num-ber 50; and Lytton, Dora, and Ralph—sometimes with Gerald, sometimes not—at number 51.

I photographed number 51 on a blustery day of intermittent sun and shadow in October. As with the dust heaps and the *Guardian*, I was questioned by a security officer. I explained my interest in the Bloomsbury Group and this house in particular, but he said that I must want the house down the square at the corner, number 46, where John Maynard Keynes lived, another Higher Sodomite whose fame is equal to Woolf's. No, it was this house I was interested in. He hadn't heard of Strachey but seemed amused when I hinted at the kind of things that had transpired there—"ladies in love with buggers and buggers in love with womanisers." He said he'd let me finish up, but I'd better be quick about it: the people who had called him from the ground floor office (the house now belongs to the Uni-versity of London) found my presence disturbing, "peculiar."

I had to hold down the tripod when the wind gusted too hard as I exposed the rest of the film in my camera. Then I traveled to the house that Strachey grew up in, hard across Hyde Park from the Albert Memorial and the childhood home of Woolf. It's part of a hotel now, as stark, tall, and forbidding as Strachey might himself have seemed on first acquaintance. But more than anything it was a blank, pure facade, empty even when it was fully booked up. I could see why Strachey hated it, shuddered at the thought of it, a stuccoed glass case that he took such care to demolish.

From there I went to number 6 Belsize Park Gardens near Hampstead. As I came up to it, I realized that I had lived directly across the street from it when I was twenty-six years old, when I might have made the high claims for my generation that Strachey made for his. I spent a couple of months there, looking for another flat to rent in another good Victorian building with a garden and high ceilings, with good shopping nearby, that would allow a cat. Nor did I have the slightest idea then who Lytton Strachey was.

I could have made—I can make—much of this: how our paths had crossed at the place where Strachey had written the bulk of *Eminent Victorians*, when I was oblivious to most of his aspirations and the vast contradictions and blindnesses that he saw in his parents' generation. I could see the irony in it, but I was at that moment mostly incapable of irony, just as the Victorians seemed to be. I was busy trying to locate solid ground, some sort of anchor amid confusion and the answer to why I was interested in them; why—and even that would do—I was standing in front of 6 Belsize Gardens.

Just then I really wanted to go to the Lake District again, the land of Mrs. Ward and of Ruskin, the place where he'd gone after Effie, when he started to come apart, when he fell in love with Rose La Touche and went mad and died a year shy of his queen. But I wasn't going to commune with either Ward or Ruskin this time but with Strachey and his ilk. In the summer of 1921 he had rented a cottage and spent August at the head of a mountain valley called Watendlath, bringing along Dora, Ralph, James, and Alix.

The previous month Gerald Brennan had returned from his hermitage in a tiny village in the Spanish hinterland. It was then that his relationship with Dora moved from flirtation to passion. Gerald was something of a naïf: it seems to have been lost on him what she meant when she wrote that she could become "very fond of two or three people" and thought of him "with great emotion." But Dora's husband, Ralph, was also more or less his best friend. Gerald tried to keep his feelings in check, though he confessed to her: "You are one of the few, almost the only, young lady (I have met few!) whom I might have fallen in love with."

In early July Gerald had managed to withstand a more direct approach from Dora at Lytton's country house: "We talked and suddenly she put her arms around me and kissed me. I let her, but afterwards felt angry because I was Ralph's friend and because she meant nothing to me." But two weeks later he returned:

> as I sat in an armchair I saw her move across the window with the evening light behind her, and I knew I was in love. It was like the first attack of flu to a Pacific Islander—I was completely, totally under from the first moment. I had fallen for her in the same way in which she had fallen for Lytton, and as violently. And she was in love with me.

Immediately after her arrival at Watendlath Dora sent him a telegram beseeching him to join her. He took the first train north.

That was fine with Ralph. He thought Gerald—lost in books and socially awkward—was harmless and would, like the rest of them, relax and do some creative work at Watendlath: "He eats, moves and sleeps, unaware of the natural laws which govern these processes. He will put anyone into a coma and withal is always interesting. Also he may very likely write a good book before he breaks his neck day-dreaming."

The Lake District was and is known for its mutable weather: drizzle and downpours, gale-force winds, cloud cover that turns day to night, but also for blasts of sunshine that arrive as epiphanies and sometimes persist. That was often the case at Watendlath that August. On those days the whole party would hike in the valley and up the mountains until Lytton's feet—sickly as the rest of his body—gave out. But rain or shine, Ralph went out to fish and Dora and Gerald followed, toting a picnic and bait. Once Ralph had settled on the bank, they would creep off to the shelter of a barn and kiss and press against one another.

That routine continued for the better part of two weeks. Gerald was enraptured but, in his guilt, wanted to confess everything to Ralph. Dora successfully persuaded him to keep their secret. Even Lytton, whose antennae were normally keenly tuned to any erotic undercurrent, wrote a friend that "so far as I can see there is precious little love-making." Every night Ralph went to sleep with Dora and in the morning was replaced in the bed by Gerald for hours of snuggling and chat.

But one day Ralph nearly caught them trysting. Dora told Gerald that he'd better leave, though she assured him later that "you can't think how I minded sending you away . . . my heart was almost breaking and my eyes crying when you left." Gerald ultimately decided, too, that it had been for the best: "I was no longer satisfied at being with you, not even kissing you—I did the only possible thing in coming away." For his part, Ralph was angry at Dora, believing that by one means or another she had driven his friend away.

Back in Spain, Gerald stewed in his regrets. "I do not want, as things are," he wrote Dora, "to be with you any longer; but to be without you is horrible. It is like going out suddenly into complete darkness." Of Watendlath he could only say it was "[m]adness, madness, horrible madness." Lytton was Lytton: "One wonders whether one has been quite wise in coming North," he wrote Virginia.

It took about forty-five minutes for me to drive the one-track road from Borrowdale to Watendlath, dodging sheep and pulling over up against the high stone walls to let the occasional car or tractor pass, much like my trip to Mrs. Ward's and *Robert Elsmere*'s Longsleddale. The landscape was much the same: May in Watendlath was not so very different from November in Longsleddale; fierce gray ridge lines shading into blue-black hills, patches of bracken, copses of disconsolate trees, exposed boulders, and a stream. But Watendlath was starker, more exposed. There were stone sheep barns, the places where Carrington and Brennan must have had their "orgy of kissing" (as Brennan put it), but otherwise little shelter. At the very end of the road was the farmhouse that Strachey and his tribe had rented, with a fence and beyond that a gate and a stone path to the front.

I thought of the triangle of Ruskin, Millais, and Effie at Glenfinlas in 1853 and of the triangle here in 1921—two overlapping triangles, really: the long-standing one involving Lytton, Ralph, and Dora and the more recent one involving Dora, Gerald, and Ralph; too complex to map. Lytton, the elder figure and organizer of the expedition, didn't quite play Ruskin in the ménage—he would have shuddered at the comparison—but he did sit inside the cottage and read and write while the others occupied themselves in and along the stream outside. He acknowledged his own libido and that of others in a way that Ruskin wouldn't or couldn't. But, as in the case of Ruskin, it took the form of observation rather than participation, analysis rather than immersion.

Strachey's take on the situation at Watendlath was amused—ironic, if you like—whereas Ruskin's was earnest. Where the Carrington-Brennan romance was in many ways farcical, the one between Effie and Millais had for me a winning charm: you cheered them on, hoping that it would all work out. By contrast, Brennan's pining for Carrington had a pathetic note, the flavor of a self-inflicted wound, what we'd characterize as a species of narcissism. Millais suffered straightforwardly, was miserable and frustrated and not quite heroic, but, for all that, was pursuing a worthy goal, a destiny. Effie-Millais feels like something from another world long ago, but Carrington-Brennan feels very much like today, like the kind of entanglements of friends and families that we're very used to, affairs that always seem to stay affairs, never reaching happy endings, trailing loose ends and ambiguous connections. Myself, I have two divorces under my belt, lovers who became friends, friends who became lovers, and people that hover in between, where regret and relief seem always to be in flux, where resolution seems likely to be always deferred.

Only sixty-eight years separate Glenfinlas from Watendlath, whereas a few years from now that summer in Watendlath will be a century ago. Yet Strachey and his cohort feel something like contemporaries. "We have liberated love," Lytton said, and what they made of it persists for many of us, more or less the status quo. I suppose I like it that way or can't imagine any other way; certainly not the way of Ruskin-Effie-Millais. It's not that I wouldn't want to—imagine the serene bliss, the steady surety of the marriage, the happy ending—but I wouldn't know how. Effie and Millais are a real-life Victorian novel that I can read but not enter into.

Reading that last sentence, I think I am admitting defeat: I was not going to find another life in the nineteenth-century, an escape from Eliot's unredeemed time. That is what I began to take in at Watendlath: with the Victorians I could go so far but then no further. At Glenfinlas I encountered no one, but at Watendlath I met people I might have known. At Glenfinlas I found a sincere and unambiguous belief in nature, art, and love; at Watendlath amorphous passions, untrustworthy forms of self-knowledge, incomprehension of others, and consolation in ironic forbearance. Ward's Longsleddale was the way station between the two, the place where faith has begun to unravel but is not quite foreclosed, might be reunderstood in ways that could sustain it. You might take Mrs. Ward's preoccupations seriously there, but by the time you get to Watendlath they had become obsolete, even ridiculous.

As at Glenfinlas, at Watendlath I had to struggle with mud and slippery rock as I took my pictures. The wind blew hard. Unlike Glenfinlas, there was no forest, no cover: only a few trees and many boulders that sometimes stood next to one another in uneasy relation. Some of the trees had put out roots toward and under and even over the rocks, a shy, tentative bid for connection, you might imagine. I let the fancy play out as I photographed one

Watendlath. Photograph by author.

such grouping: was the boulder irritated or indifferent to the tree's approach or just tongue-tied, as stone must be? The tree would never know and of course in the end the boulder would out-live it. Maybe other trees would come and then go in the same way with no more clarity than the one I was photographing. Such is life in Watendlath.

"One wonders whether one has been quite wise in coming North," Lytton wrote when the holiday ended. Ralph went back to Spain with his tail between his legs, and the rest of them returned to London and its often appalling, unfathomable people, one foot in the Victorian grave, the other hesitantly in the post-1910 dispensation. As Lytton recorded, "Mrs. Arnold Bennett recited with waving arms and chanting voice Baudelaire and Verlaine until everyone was ready to vomit. As a study in half-witted horror the whole thing was most interesting."

In my life, people don't recite much poetry, certainly not while waving their arms. We're beyond that now, I think, as was Lytton; we have to be, whether we want to be or not. We crossed the boundary into Woolf's December 1910 then World War I; maybe love in the mode of Watendlath put the seal on it. When I'd gone to London I hadn't figured on that. I was aiming for Glenfinlas, Dickens's and Gissing's Clerkenwell, St. Pancras Station, or just Riceyman Steps/Gwynne Place—the real and the imagined nicely overlapping—but woke up in Bloomsbury by way of Swinton Street.

Chapter 5

IN THE SPRING of 2015 I returned to America and moved to New York. Once I was settled there, I flew back to England. I had a list of to-dos—photos to take, places to revisit—and then I would be done. I wanted to be done. The tasks were essentially Victorian ones: collecting yet more specimens, hoarding more bric-a-brac, turning memory and loss into totems to mourn or, if that was unbearable, sentimentalize. I hadn't lost interest in the Victorians, but now that was all they were—an interest. They weren't going to save me.

I put the list on my phone, on my calendar, intending to do at least one location per day or sometimes two.

Staplehurst Crash Site (Dickens/*Our Mutual Friend*)
22 Hyde Park Gate (Leslie Stephen/Virginia Woolf)
18 Melbury Rd (Holman Hunt)
Northampton General Lunatic Asylum (George Gilbert Scott Jr.)

St. Pancras Hotel (George Gilbert Scott Sr. and Jr.)
Swinton Street

I'd brought fourteen rolls of film and given myself a week to get through it. I thought that would be enough, but things began to go wrong. Photography, as often was the case, seemed to want to frustrate me; to bring me up short. In Staplehurst I got lost. When I found the bridge over the railway line that overlooked the crash site, the walls on either side were higher than the reach of my tripod. I had to hold the camera above my head and shoot blind, hoping some sort of composition would fall into place. Then it began to rain. I didn't have an umbrella, so I had to shelter under a tree until it stopped. I was damp, my feet hurt, I'd made slapdash photos, and I wondered why I'd come: why, really, any of this was important.

At the home of Leslie Stephen and his daughters, I found other obstacles. It was in a high-rent neighborhood whose oligarch residents were constantly remodeling, gutting Victorian interiors to install underground swimming pools and multicar garages. Buildings were obscured by scaffolding or board fences. At the Stephen house, people (mostly construction workers) wouldn't move out of my frame. Parked cars blocked the view. Rain swept in just as I set up my camera.

Similarly, everything I wanted to photograph in Swinton Street seemed to be obscured by traffic or parked cars. And, more essentially, I could not summon up the sense of my panic there nine months before: it was irreproducible—my conviction that catastrophe was upon me—something that happened outside the spectrum of any film stock or the resolution of any lens.

George Gilbert Scott Junior's places gave me less trouble. I took the train to the Northampton General Lunatic Asylum on a squally Sunday afternoon. The name is now simply St. Andrew's Hospital, although it is still a psychiatric facility. Virginia Woolf's cousin John Stephen had been a patient here too, contemporaneously with George Scott Jr., committed for the same manic-depression

Sir George Gilbert Scott, St. Andrew's Hospital Chapel.
Photograph by author.

that Virginia was afflicted with, which ran in her family, as with
Turner and Ruskin and so many others.

The grounds were beautiful, a classical terrace of wards overlooking a vast lawn. When I arrived a dozen or so people were playing croquet, patients, I supposed. At the lawn's far edge I saw the
chapel that Scott Junior's father designed. It would be visible from
any of the wards, so Scott could have seen it whenever he looked
out. I wondered what that was like for him: this manifestation of
his father's incessant productivity and mastery of the conventions
of Victorian Gothic that Scott Junior had not fully succeeded in
overturning. Or maybe it made no impression because his expe-

rience was by then entirely internal, a knot of paranoid fantasy. People were trying to poison him, assassins had been hired; he had more pressing things to worry about than the insult and accusations of his father's chapel.

Or maybe—and this is how I believed it must have been—he'd look out and the chapel would stare back, shaming him. Alcoholics are habituated to shame, as are sons of eminent men (maybe all sons to some extent). There were trees around the chapel, big conifers that cast pools and rivulets of light flowing in the direction of the wards. Gazing out, Scott Junior would have seen them approaching, serpentine, mirroring what he'd conjured up in his own brain.

He had no choice about being committed to St. Andrew's, but in his next and final home he embraced the same dialectic—son and father, art and shame—even more profoundly, taking a room inside the St. Pancras Hotel, deep within his father's oeuvre, swallowed up by it until what proved to be the very end.

Almost all the photos of St. Andrew's came out underexposed; the shifting light played tricks on my light meter—or that is how I excused myself from the failure. That's what I would have told anyone who might take me to task me for it; those who would present themselves as older and wiser and would say that I hadn't taken the time to master the craft; that I was careless and immature; that I needed to listen and learn, to stop living in a fantasy world. And now I am thinking of an extract from General Gordon's diary that Strachey had mentioned, written as the enemy was beginning its siege of Khartoum—the things that were on Gordon's mind as he was preparing to die:

The splendid hawks that swooped about the palace reminded [Gordon] of a text in the Bible: "The eye that mocketh at his father and despiseth to obey his mother, the ravens of the valley shall pick it out, and the young eagles shall eat it." "I often wonder," he wrote, "whether they are destined to pick my eyes, for I fear I was not the best of sons."

One of the crucial things that separated Strachey's generation from the Victorians was their indifference to the opinions and regard of their fathers, in fact, making a virtue of rejecting most of what their fathers thought most important. It seemed to them self-evident that those fathers' posterity culminated in nothing so much as the slaughter of the 1914–1918 war. Their fathers were in deadly earnest; held to deadly sureties that sent their sons and grandsons to the trenches. The ravens would come whether anyone deserved it or not.

Returning to London, I had two places left to photograph. Holman Hunt's villa in Melbury Road seemed scarcely worth bothering with, as it was almost completely hidden by scaffolds and tarpaulins. But I needed to see where Virginia Woolf had gone on her misbegotten debutante night out and, still more, to fathom my perplexity about Hunt, to embrace or dismiss him once and for all; I couldn't, it seemed, be done with this whole business until I'd done that. I could see the front door in the shadow of the scaffold. Somewhere above it, veiled in boards and tenting, was the studio where he'd held forth that night in his gentle manner, swaddled in the glow of *The Light of the World*.

Woolf hadn't said what she thought of the painting; she was observing the Victorian monument of the man himself. For myself, I had got a copy of what seemed to be his only biography, by A. C. Gissing. I realized that he must be Alfred Gissing, the younger son of George Gissing. He had been his father's favorite, the one of whom Gissing had written, "I always felt guilty of a crime in abandoning the poor little fellow." That was when Gissing had run off to France, leaving Alfred and his older brother to be raised on a farm in Cornwall and sent to boarding school. Like almost every son in his generation, Alfred went into the army in 1914, serving in India, where he was out of harm's way; his older brother, Walter, like so many other sons, was killed in the Battle of Somme.

After discharge, Alfred worked as a teacher and headmaster. He had money from his father's estate as well as the proceeds of an honorary government pension arranged by H. G. Wells and his father's other literary friends. The royalties from George Gissing's books gradually increased. From the 1930s onward Alfred mostly occupied himself managing the estate and editing his father's miscellaneous works. Sometimes he wrote to the *Times* when an anecdote or supposed fact about his father needed correcting, but he seemed to live a leisured life. He was, in effect, a son with a trust fund.

I don't know what moved Alfred Gissing to write a biography of Holman Hunt in 1935: there's no evidence that he thought of himself as an art historian or connoisseur. I can't imagine that he did it for the money, as he had never shown any inclination to aim for commercial success. So I suppose he simply liked Hunt very much indeed. Perhaps—because his book didn't persuade me to adopt the same attitude—I can't be fair to him. But when I read it, it did not seem to be a very good book. The sentences were competently made and the research thorough. But most of the time it read like this:

He was, at the moment now reached by our history, in his twenty-eighth year and, precarious though his resources undoubtedly were, the breadth of his experience, his indomitable courage, his genius, his rocklike sincerity formed a foundation beneath his feet from which adversity could not easily move him. Not that in another age he might not have shared the fortunes of artists, but despite the insults of the mob . . . he was yet saved by the leaven of society from the worst sufferings of an artist's life.

The book was an exercise in fulsome admiration, less a view of a life than a collection of anecdotes—many of them dubious—designed to illustrate its hero's progress by dint of pluck, moral fortitude, and dogged labor to his well-deserved niche in the pantheon of genius. The book's eye—proceeding sentence by fussy sentence, each one insisting on its protagonist's high character—

was forever on the moral of its story. There wasn't a word about the drama at Glenfinlas in 1853 (to say nothing of Hunt's proposal to Virginia Woolf's mother). While Millais was acknowledged as Hunt's best friend, Alfred Gissing cast him as a much inferior artist who abandoned the true Pre-Raphaelite faith to make himself rich as a society painter.

The book contains nothing of Alfred's father's style either: "the impression that it leaves of a live human creature who has not scrupled to let us know his foibles and his failings, and his imperfect human shape," as Virginia Woolf wrote in her review of George Gissing's final novel, *The Private Papers of Henry Ryecroft*. Needless to say, it contained nothing of Lytton Strachey's rethinking of biography and reappraisal of the Victorian character. And there was nothing in it to make me like *The Light of the World*. As a writer, it was Hunt himself that I came to admire a bit, from quotations of his diaries, descriptions of "look[ing] over the gunwale into the lapis-lazuli water, dense as in a dyer's vat, marbled all through with engulfing veins."

Alfred Gissing, it seemed to me, was a Victorian writer living in 1935, minus the doubt, conflict, and tenuous hopes that the best Victorian writers struggled with: what money did and didn't do; what class and gender meant; what the consequences of technology, urbanization, and advanced capitalism might be; how or if faith and doubt could be squared. In that, I thought Strachey was wrong about "their refusal to face any fundamental question fairly—either about people or God— . . . an innate incapacity for penetration—for getting either out of themselves or into anything or anyone else." That wasn't true of George Gissing or any of my Victorians. What was true, though, was that there was no going back. Admiring Holman Hunt as the Victorians themselves did— as Alfred Gissing did—seemed a kind of betrayal of the present, of the people we'd become in their wake—much more, as Woolf intuited, the kind of "imperfect human shapes" that the elder Gissing had penetrated and that his son had not.

I couldn't, though, agree with Woolf about Bennett. Maybe I needed him as what D. W. Winnicott called a "transitional object," the toddler's blanket or stuffed toy that serves as a way station between the paradoxical omnipotence and dependence of the infant's world and the acquisition of the sense of self and other that constitutes our first move toward full personhood. Bennett's steps and Bennett the writer were halfway between my Victorians and Woolf's Bloomsbury; *Riceyman Steps* and Gwynne Place led, it seemed to me, from an ordered, shaded nineteenth-century square to the anodyne buildings and roar of traffic below; to post-Victorian anxiety and boredom; to being always and everywhere of two or three minds; to there being altogether too much world and too little that could be known and taken on faith.

After I'd taken all the photos on my list, I had one day left before going home to America and my new home in New York. I went to Riceyman Steps/Gwynne Place. Though I was done with the list, I took my camera.

It was autumn: leaves were heaped up, huddled at the base of the steps, and, to their left, a large gate that I'd never seen open before. Inside was a large space that had once formed the back-yards of the seven or eight Victorian houses—still standing—facing onto Granville Square above, the walls between them vanished, the ground paved with concrete. I heard the Metropolitan underground line rumbling beneath it—the first subway in the world, one of the great Victorian projects in London—on its way to St. Pancras.

I realized that this expanse would have been the site of the yard where Elsie in *Riceyman Steps* heard a dog howling and then saw a beautiful woman come out of the house—where "behind that window someone was suffering and someone was watching"—into the yard and beat the dog into silence.

The dog had haunted me as wolves used to do when I was a small child, as the memory of my terror of them still sometimes did: the terror, really, of the terror itself, of things going wrong—crashes, uncertainties, ambiguities. I pictured the dog howling and pacing in the thick, damp night; the pretty, furious woman, and then the blows falling and the whimpers, all this a century and a quarter ago. Of course, there'd never been such a dog, or not this dog anyway, which was a product of Bennett's imagination; nor had there been the beautiful woman or, for that matter, an Elsie to see her, to imagine the other occupants of her house, suffering or sleepless in the night. There was no observer except me, looking at what never was.

I set up my camera and made half a dozen exposures of the long yard visible through the half-opened gate. The concrete ran up to the rear walls of the houses, pressed up to the base of a cliff of brick and empty windows, towering, moldering. In three trips to Britain over the last two years, I'd taken nearly a thousand—984 exactly—photographs of Victorian buildings and places. When I got back to New York and the darkroom, I saw that these final pictures were the best of all. I saw that the measure and nature of my obsession was most present, most palpable, in these bare pictures of imagined remains, of nothing; nothing, really, at all.

That afternoon, I went to the Tate Britain, the old Tate on Millbank that's now a little forgotten, overshadowed by the huge Tate Modern downstream. It's named for Henry Tate, the magnate who founded Tate and Lyle and made refined sugar the staple ingredient of the Victorian diet. It's now dedicated entirely to British art (the foreign and modern collections have been moved to the Modern) and especially to Turner. During my two years of research and photography, I never paid much attention to Turner: he wasn't really a Victorian painter. Practically speaking, he lived only fourteen years into Victoria's reign, but on the other hand he also had his greatest advocate in the young John Ruskin, who championed Turner's much derided and misunderstood work. But it was Ruskin's other, later advocacy that occupied me at the Tate: the painters who had become famous—Millais and Hunt, most prominently—after Turner's death in 1851, who had, it seemed to me, emerged out of the summer of 1853.

I knew the layout of the museum well and the locations of the favorite paintings I'd been revisiting every few years for three decades: William Hogarth's *Servants*, John Singer Sargent's *Carnation, Lily, Lily, Rose*, Stanley Spencer's self-portraits, David Hockney's *Mr. and Mrs. Clark and Percy*. I'd looked at the Turners as well but with less enthusiasm. I see now that they required more of me; they did not explain themselves; they met you halfway and no further. Someday I'll try to fathom them.

That afternoon I went straight to the Victorians. They had been my familiars for the last five years, the touchstones of my obsession, but this time I didn't linger over any one painting. I strolled through the gallery at a clip, not much more than skimming them: John William Waterhouse's *Lady of Shalott*, three or four by Burne-Jones, and then Millais and Hunt. I stopped for those, wondering what I'd make of them, wondering if they would draw me in or trouble me now; if my fascination was intact. It had never been about loving or unreservedly admiring any of them; I knew that Turner was the better painter. I knew that Ruskin could be very right about some things but perverse about others.

I stopped at Millais's *Mariana*. A year ago I had associated it with Effie Ruskin and the way Millais had posed her at Doune Castle in 1853. I could still see Mariana's frank eroticism, but what I noticed now were the maple leaves scattered around her feet. I'd never seen them before and wondered what they meant; they had to symbolize something allegorical or iconographic just as everything in Pre-Raphaelite art had to. As that thought slipped away, another replaced it: I was convinced that Mariana's feet were bare or must be bare, although I couldn't see them, hidden as they are by her long blue dress. I wondered about that: I could see that she was a legend, but I wanted to know if she was human; if, under and beyond the symbols, her feet might get muddy as Effie's had; if she could be touched.

Hunt's *The Awakening Conscience* was close by. The reflected window was still the best thing about it, the faces and heads the worst, just as in *The Light of the World*. *The Awakening Conscience* was probably just as off-putting, but it was satisfied to be no more

than a moralizing painting, while *The Light of the World* was playing for higher stakes: for redemption and eternity. If it did its job
fully, it might have made a huge dent in Victorian agnosticism.
The painting had reaffirmed the faith of millions on its world
tour, though it couldn't stop the steady creep of doubt that the
current of history was driving onward.

The painting itself was off in Oxford, but even at a distance it
remained an irritation that created a doubt about my doubt, an
uneasy superstition about my convictions. Suppose the beckon-
ing figure, tiny head and all, was daring me to consider what was
under offer; suppose I was wrong and he was right? For reasons
that made no sense, the awfulness of the painting didn't make it
easier to dismiss. Perhaps that was because another kind of faith
was also at stake: the conviction that my Victorian obsession was
worth anything or was, like the painting, a laughable, sentimental
folly. But I was close to deciding: the painting was awful, beautiful
for Victorians, in the way that Ruskin had taught them, but useless, even repellent, for me. I would never see what they saw in it. It
belonged to them.

I saw that the room that contained the Millais and the Hunt
had some new things in its far corner. This part of the collection
had been rehung to produce a timeline of British art, not a com-
partmentalization of periods room by room: twenty feet from the
Pre-Raphaelites hung twentieth-century works that were new to
me. One was a slab of stone, inscribed in Latin "EX DIVINA PUL-
CHRITUDINE ESSE OMNIUM DERIVATUR." It had been carved
by the sculptor and typographer Eric Gill, who designed several
exquisite typefaces still much in use and whose sculptures were
incorporated into the fabric of BBC Broadcasting House and
Westminster Cathedral. He was a fervent convert to Catholicism,
and the inscription here, a quotation from Saint Thomas Aquinas,
suited him both as an artist and as a believer: "The beauty of God
is the cause of the being of all that is." I could accept this propo-
sition as I could never accept Christ's in *The Light of the World*. It
could be read in the abstract: "God" could be whatever entity or

force or idea you liked; it could be construed circularly as the simple principle of Beauty: God is Beauty and Beauty is God. I could happily assent to that; it was harmless, made no demands, caused no disruptions, required no submission to a father God. The carving was undeniably beautiful, which could also be bracketed off from a larger, more complicated context. Gill was a devout Catholic who was also a multiple and active pedophile, whose victims included his own children. That was harder to bracket. Gill had gone down the path that Ruskin, so far as we know, only imagined. They'd both pledged themselves to beauty and the givenness of things, Gill to *pulchritudine* (whence the English "pulchritude"), Ruskin to the imperative "You shall see things as they Are." But in this case I wouldn't look too closely.

Farther along the wall, at the corner, was a small painting, perhaps two feet square. I'd never seen it before; nor did I know it was owned by the Tate. It was, I saw, by Dora Carrington and was called *Farm at Watendlath*. It would have been painted in August when she was entangled with Gerald Brennan and Ralph Partridge, with Lytton Strachey looking on, when everything was "at sixes and sevens." She'd softened the hills, pushed the buildings together into a cozy intimacy, sheets strung between the trees to dry, and put a woman walking hand in hand with a child in the middle distance. There hadn't been any children at Watendlath, so that part was imagined. Of course, Carrington and Gerald had in their fashion been like children there; they had "liberated love," as Lytton had put it. Lytton, of course, would have had no use for anything from Arnold Bennett, but Bennett had reminded himself in his *Riceyman Steps* notebook always to remember that his protagonist "confused love and dream." I think that may have been true of Watendlath and still is everywhere. It is where I find myself living, having forsaken Ruskin and all the others. I'd imagined, as Gerald wrote Dora, that being without them "[would be] like going out suddenly into complete darkness," but the feeling wasn't wrenching or devastating; my Victorians had quietly withdrawn, receded into something very much like Matthew Arnold's "sea of faith." I turned around on the shore and saw that, together with their God, they had gone.

That my interest in the Victorians is now no larger than any other interest of mine is, in retrospect, not surprising, though it seemed a very sudden alteration. One moment I had been obsessed—in a romance that was also a dream—and the next, photographing those last few places, I knew that I'd ceased to care. The Victorians and I were friends, but no more than that.

Another Victorian, Oscar Wilde, said, "We teach people how to remember, we never teach them how to grow." It's possible that I put all the impulses that I had once used for growth into remembering. Perhaps I imagined that if I went deep enough into the world of the books I loved, I'd be happy; I'd be at home in another place and time, as though I'd died and gone to another realm, escaping the things I feared were pursuing me: shame, love, adulthood, death. I'd be a ghost to the present, haunting the twenty-first century rather than inhabiting it.

But just as sentimentality is a replica of genuine feeling, fossilizing rather than grieving the raw, unprocessed material of memory, such a life could be only a replica of living. Because the past is for us always a failure. We are here, and it is there. The gap cannot be unmade with the longest, most faithful leap or even, perhaps, in the imagination. We will always fall short of it, miss the mark. I don't upbraid myself for putting so much into my Victorians and not coming away with what I wanted. It's nothing to be ashamed of. I have a thousand photographs and these words. I have the traces and relics, not, as I'd aimed, of the Victorians but of my time pursuing them, five years in this world, not theirs.

But I still have something of them, or aspects of them, in myself: their earnestness and good cheer and willingness to wrestle with the devil when the devil arguably doesn't exist. And I still have their purblindness, the inability to penetrate into my own heart or know my own thoughts (as Strachey, half-right, said), or even into what they clearly said—and still say, when I pick up a book or look at St. Pancras Station. Take Ruskin, who epitomized sexual confusion, the psychologically unexamined self, loss of faith, incessant and perhaps pointless labor ending in what we'd call hypergraphia. He was a fool but also a true visionary—everything was all vision for Ruskin. He proposed nothing like the modern or postmodern worldview but something altogether more alien and strange and, I think, necessary: his call to engage nature— the eternally present moment—rather than the historical past, personal or public. "You shall see things as they Are," not as they were or might be.

It's all in the particulars, in the present particular and only there: Ruskin's "awful" and its companion beauty, maybe even Aquinas's "divina pulchritudine," the God that got lost. But Ruskin was not speaking of anything deliberately grand or self-regardingly profound. He was only interested in making art and culture formed with what was ready to hand: nature or even industrial Britain: "If we are now to do anything great, good, awful, religious, it must be got out of our own little island, and out of this year 1846, railroads and all." Ruskin hated railroads, that most Victorian of Victorian inventions, but he understood what could be and needed to be made with them.

Still, Ruskin moved to the Lake District, among other reasons, to escape the noise and smoke of trains, and it was there he went mad and died. Visitors can stay in an apartment in his house there, Brantwood, and I spent the night in it five years ago, just as my Victoromania was first emerging. When the house was closed to the public at the end of the day and the staff went home, I was entirely alone. You're not allowed to wander the halls, but you can see the cupola where Ruskin often wrote, which is illumined by a lamp that burns all night. I thought that would be spooky and was wondering how it would make me feel, knowing that Ruskin raved and pined and died there.

But nothing like that happened. I heated a frozen dinner and watched a movie on my laptop. I sensed no presences and heard no whispers. I was firmly cemented in 2011, which is how in 1846 Ruskin would have insisted I be. The house in 1846 had been his;

this house with convenience food and Netflix, uninhabited by the past, was mine.

The intimation was lost on me then. I left first thing in the morning in haste, not out of unease, but to catch a train. I didn't know it then, but Watendlath was close by. I may even have driven past the road that ascends to it. But I didn't get there for another four years; and when I did, I would have only my moment, not, really, the moment of Strachey or any of his ilk. It was only way station, there and then gone. Failure or not, I've come through unscathed. I may, *pace* Oscar Wilde, even have grown. I got from Glenfinlas to Watendlath, so there isn't far to go until I find myself here, where I am now, still—inevitably—at sixes and sevens.

Here and now is New York City. I left Seattle when I realized that all along I had been intending to go somewhere else for good, that I was in flight, and that it would not be the nineteenth century or even, for practical considerations, London. Nothing and no one was waiting there for me: just as with my Victorians, I had formed no deep friendships and never quite connected with any of the women I'd dated. That was just as well: like Ruskin's nearly featureless sketch of Effie, I couldn't truly make them out; and they perhaps sensed that, wherever I was, it was not entirely with them.

New York suits me—I know that I am a creature of cities—but, like London, also has ghosts. I have fears of things that aren't dependable in the way a Victorian novel is dependable—and some of them go back a long way. Terrified by Sergei Prokofiev's *Peter and the Wolf*, I began to conjure wolves in the basement and its dark places and, in the night, in my room. My fear extended to canines in general, to dogs, which might chase or lunge at me (in fairness to my five-year-old self, they had done so and given me some bites too). I was also anxious about marine life with claws, especially the crabs in Cape Cod Bay near my father's house after my parents' divorce. I was worried that I'd get pinched, though it never happened. Disasters, larger in scope, far from my home and outside my experience, and incomprehensible to my undeveloped grasp of cause and effect or human error, preoccupied me even more: you could avoid dogs, wolves, and crabs, but catastrophes came out of nowhere and couldn't be evaded or hidden from.

On December 16, 1960, a United Airlines DC-8 with eighty-four passengers had crashed at about 10:30 in the morning at the intersection of Sterling Place and Seventh Avenue in Park Slope, Brooklyn. It had collided over Staten Island with another airliner carrying a further forty-four people. I remember the TV saying that the accident took place over New York harbor and pictured the two planes falling into the sea, shreds of aluminum pouring out of the clouds, bodies like snowflakes—it had been snowing thickly enough that you couldn't see, enough that the planes were flying on instruments—or maybe the planes were intact, spiraling down, human faces at the windows, diving beneath the surface.

In fact, the Constellation fell onto Staten Island, and the DC-8 remained airborne for several miles before crashing in Brooklyn. The DC-8 received most of the press attention: it carried the bulk of the victims; it was a state-of-the-art airplane, just-introduced, the pure incarnation of America's "jet age." In the midst of a New York City street its wreckage—especially the fully intact tail section that came to rest squarely at the intersection of Sterling Place and Seventh Avenue—produced arresting, incongruous images.

It also contained the only passenger found alive at either crash site, an eleven-year-old boy who'd been seated near the tail and was apparently thrown clear of the wreckage onto a snowbank in front of a bodega. He was badly burned, his face so blackened that the passersby who discovered and tended him couldn't make out what race he was. He'd been put on the plane alone in Chicago to meet his mother for a family vacation in New York. His name was Stephen Baltz, and he was a boy something like me.

Stephen would say that he'd heard a loud noise and then the plane was falling; he worried that his mother, waiting for him at the airport, wouldn't know where he was. He was a sort of everyboy: curious, midwestern, middle-class, a Boy Scout and Little

Leaguer. He raised hamsters and built model planes. Once settled in his hospital room, he asked if he could have a television set to watch. The day he boarded the DC-8 he had sixty-five cents (mostly in nickels) in his pocket. When he died—not from the burns, but of pneumonia from the jet fuel that had coated his lungs—his father put the money in the hospital poor box.

The crash—the worst in American history up to that time— made a huge impression on me: ordinary life, I saw, could go terribly, inexplicably wrong. The usual state of affairs—things as they always were and always should be—could collapse and crash, could do so a thousand miles away, unbeknownst to you as you sat in school, right over your head. Things could be *this* way, and unalterably so. It was—I only remember this now—less than a year after my father's death.

I hadn't thought of the crash in years, at least not since its fiftieth anniversary in 2010, when it had received some coverage in the *New York Times*; the year I'd begun chasing my Victorians. Now it was 2015 and I'd moved to Brooklyn and I found myself, not quite aware of any intention, walking toward Sterling Place. I knew where I was headed, of course, and at the same time was asking myself: Are you really going there? To gawk, to indulge your morbid curiosity? But by then I was nearly to the intersection where the wreckage had fallen. I held back a hundred feet short of it. I needed to get my bearings. I got out my phone and Googled up some crash photos and the scene began to unveil itself, the buildings arranging themselves in my eye. What I had needed was the compass needle of the tail-section looming in the intersection, the charred membranes of aluminum, the desiccated winter light that illumined the snowbank in front of the bodega where Stephen Baltz had lain.

I walked toward the corner, confident I could toggle my view back and forth from 1960 to the present, that I could place what I'd imagined atop what I saw and they'd align correctly. The intersection was identical in most of its particulars, save for the buildings that had been destroyed in the impact and fire. I stopped there for what seemed a very long time, though it was perhaps all of thirty seconds. I became conscious that I myself might be standing out to others; that they would see a man in a long dark coat lingering inappropriately on the corner in a city where people famously do not linger unless they are up to no good. And I was up to no good: I was a prurient rubbernecker, ghoulishly enthralled by what was none of my business, by the dead who should be left in peace, ghosts who should not be haunted by the living.

But it was a past that felt essential to me, even if it was a past over which I had no rights. I felt the pervert's shame at his irresistible fascination—his compulsion to own what he knows is not his—and I unaccountably remembered Fascination Fledgeby in *Our Mutual Friend*, who exploits people's greed and penury, their desire, but also their simplest needs. Maybe someone would see me from an apartment window, would call the police, who would take me, a petty thief of other people's tragedy, to Riker's Island, where I'd be victimized by the people who belonged to this city, who had a right to all its suffering.

I turned around and skittered down the block toward the subway as though pursued. But I halted midway. I knew that this was my one chance to see the crash site; that I wouldn't come back and wouldn't need to if I once and for all took hold of it, comprehended it. So I returned to the intersection and tried to fathom what the missing piece was, the thing that was out of place. I stared hard and ceased to worry about being noticed. I was on a mission just as I had been in England: this mattered to me in a way that other people couldn't begin to comprehend.

I looked diagonally across to the southwest corner where the bodega stood. The building seemed the same as in the photos, but there was something wrong about the roof. Someone had built a cupola on it, a covered deck five stories above Stephen Baltz's snowbank. I looked up at the roof, at the vantage point it possessed, and then down at the sidewalk and the curb. And there he is, the boy who fell from the sky, smut-faced as a chimney

Backyard adjacent to Gwynne Place, site of the barking dog in *Riceyman Steps*. Photograph by author.

sweep, and you couldn't even say if he were white, if he had any business in this neighborhood, with a suitcase fallen next to him, as though he'd brought luggage along. Of course, he's still a child, a Peter Pan; he'll never grow up, he'll miss the 1960s and all the rest, the misgivings and nostalgic unease that I have; the sense, really, of not having grown up either.

I looked up again. No one was there, or maybe Jenny Wren was. She was on the rooftop, the better to see things: "You see the clouds rushing on above the narrow streets, not minding them, and you see the golden arrows pointing at the mountains in the

sky from which the wind comes, and you feel as if you were dead."
Yes, she sees: the clouds of smoke and snow, the narrow streets
beneath, the cooling wreckage, and the crossbar of the aircraft's
broken tail. " 'Oh, so tranquil!' cried the little creature, smiling.
'Oh, so peaceful and so thankful! And you hear the people who
are alive, crying and working, and calling to one another down in
the close dark streets, and you seem to pity them so!' " She might
be seeing me. I turned back toward the subway but stopped and
looked back two or three times. I might have been Fledgeby, who
"heard the sweet little voice, more and more faintly, half calling
and half singing, 'Come back and be dead, Come back and be
dead!' "

Now I live permanently in Brooklyn and pass by the intersection
on occasion, always wondering why I'm there, even if it's the obvious route from A to B, wondering if I have some ulterior motive.
But I am mostly puzzled by why I remained so focused on the
crash when there is so much more immediate, surpassing horror in the world happening right now. It's a failure, surely, of both
compassion and imagination, which are perhaps only, after all,
the same thing.

But as a Victorian, Gerard Manley Hopkins, said, the world is
charged with the grandeur of God. I think we only see as much
of it as we can bear; we pick and choose, none of us quite the
same things. And just as with God—because of God—the world
is charged with meaning, more than anyone can deal with; but
the loss of any shred of it will be devastating to someone, which
is to say that the world's also charged with loss, which carries off
meaning with it and, we fear, everything that we love; everything
that can love us.

For a long time I thought I'd found a stay against loss, pledging
I'd never let tragedy lay a finger on me, but the plane had been following me—or I couldn't let it go. That was the fascination, my
mouth agape before catastrophe, but also getting off scot-free,
shillings and pence ringing in my pockets:

Thus Fascination Fledgeby went his way, exulting in the artful cleverness with which he had turned his thumb down on a Jew, and . . . the call or song began to sound in his ears again, and looking above, he saw the face of the little creature looking down out of a Glory of her long bright radiant hair, and musically repeating to him, like a vision: "Come up and be dead! Come up and be dead!"

My view of the hereafter or its ineffable intrusions into the present, as confused and diffident as any Victorian's, can't make any sense of that scene's icily unsentimental cosmology or of the indifferent God that I'd assembled from the debris of my faith: the difficult, cussed God with his heartbreaking algebras: grandeur minus loss equals tragedy, which equals what seems to me zero, null. But perhaps he bequeaths to me what is just shy of that—fears that stop short of annihilation, of total loss, but are kept always suspended before my eyes, an inheritance—not past but present—that can't be avoided or renounced. He sent Jenny Wren to call me to be dead, so that I might err in my own way and perhaps stumble into the now, into redeemed time; and say to her, if I liked, "No, not yet."

ACKNOWLEDGMENTS

First, my gratitude to James McCoy and Meredith Stabel, who took this book through publication with enthusiasm, patience, and unstinting commitment. For their kindness, support, and forbearance, endless thanks to Emily Ash and John Benbow, Jeffrey Eaton, Margaret Friedman, Patricia Hampl, Peter Juvonen, David Shields, Lauren Winner, Gregory Wolfe, and the Wallingford Center writers; my love to Andrew, Jeremy, Millie, Tessa, and Theo; and to Jeffery Smith, *requiescas in pace*, dear friend.

SELECTED BIBLIOGRAPHY

Annan, Noel. *Leslie Stephen: The Godless Victorian*. Chicago: University of Chicago Press, 1984.

Bennett, Arnold. "Notebook for Riceyman Steps." Arnold Bennett Collection of Papers, 1881–1955. New York Public Library, Berg Collection, Berg Coll MSS Bennett.

Cotsell, Michael. *The Companion to "Our Mutual Friend."* New York: Routledge, 2014.

Coustillas, Pierre. *The Heroic Life of George Gissing, Part I: 1857–1886*. London: Pickering & Chatto, 2011.

———. *The Heroic Life of George Gissing, Part II: 1888–1897*. London: Pickering & Chatto, 2012.

———. *The Heroic Life of George Gissing, Part III: 1897–1903*. London: Pickering & Chatto, 2012.

Coustillas, Pierre, ed. *London and the Life of Literature in Late Victorian England: The Diary of George Gissing, Novelist*. Hassocks, Sussex: Harvester, 1978.

Davis, Philip. *The Victorians*. Oxford: Oxford University Press, 2002.

Dickens Our Mutual Friend Reading Project, Birkbeck College, London. January 21, 2016. https://dickensourmutualfriend.wordpress.com.

Douglas-Fairhurst, Robert. *Becoming Dickens: The Invention of a Novelist*. Cambridge, MA: Belknap, 2011.

———. *The Story of Alice: Lewis Carroll and the Secret History of Wonderland*. Cambridge, MA: Belknap, 2015.

Emerson, Ralph Waldo. *The Journals and Miscellaneous Notebooks of Ralph Waldo Emerson*. Edited by William Gilman et al. Cambridge, MA: Belknap Press, 1960.

Garnett, Robert. *Dickens in Love*. Berkeley, CA: Pegasus, 2013.

Gissing, A. C. *William Holman Hunt: A Biography*. London: Duckworth, 1936.

Hawthorne, Nathaniel. *The English Notebooks: Nathaniel Hawthorne*. Edited by Thomas Woodson and Bill Ellis. Columbus: Ohio State University Press, 1997.

Hill, Rosemary. *God's Architect: Pugin and the Building of Romantic Britain*. London: Allen Lane, 2007.

Hilton, Tim. *John Ruskin: The Early Years, 1819–1859*. New Haven, CT: Yale University Press, 1985.

———. *John Ruskin: The Later Years*. New Haven, CT: Yale University Press, 2000.

Holroyd, Michael. *Lytton Strachey: The New Biography*. London: Chatto & Windus, 1994.

Lee, Hermione. *Virginia Woolf*. London: Chatto & Windus, 1996.

Lutyens, Elizabeth. *Millais and the Ruskins*. Edinburgh: Murray, 1967.

Lutyens, Elizabeth, and Malcolm Warner. *Rainy Days at Brig O'Turk: The Highland Sketchbooks of John Everett Millais, 1853*. Westerham, Kent: Dalrymple, 1983.

Maas, Jeremy. *Holman Hunt and The Light of the World*. London: Scolar, 1984.

Mattheisen, Paul F., Arthur C. Young, and Pierre Coustillas eds. *The Collected Letters of George Gissing*. Athens: Ohio University Press, 1990–1996.

Stamp, Gavin. *An Architect of Promise: George Gilbert Scott Jr and the Late Gothic Revival*. Donington, Lincolnshire: Shaun Tyas, 2002.

Strachey, Lytton. *The Letters of Lytton Strachey*. Edited by Paul Levy. London: Penguin, 2005.

Sutherland, John. *The Longman Companion to Victorian Fiction*. 2nd ed. London: Pearson Education, 2009.

———. *Mrs Humphry Ward: Eminent Victorian, Pre-eminent Edwardian*. Oxford: Oxford University Press, 1991.